Spiritual Songs II:

BLESSINGS FROM A
SACRED SOUL

Ann Marie Ruby

To the Little Free Library
Enjoy reading!
With love,
Ann Marie Ruby

Published in The United States of America, 2019.

ISBN-10: 0-578-45558-7

ISBN-13: 978-0-578-45558-7

DEDICATION

Sacred blessing for all humankind is but humanity. For humanity, we the humans exist. From the beginning of time, through the present days, we have won the war within ourselves. The biggest victory of all time is known as humanity. For this reason, we feed the hungry. We build shelters for the homeless. We walk into war zones and treat the wounded.

Bridging all differences between the humans for the sake of humanity, is the blessed achievement of the wise. Within this life, there is only one gift and for me, that is humanity. No race, color, or religion will ever prevent me from holding the hands of a sick, injured, or helpless child. No land or border on Earth will prevent me from holding on to another soul. This sacred soul will sing the tunes of humanity throughout eternity.

Today, I dedicate my sacred book to all humans across this globe who believe in one race, one color, and one religion, for these are but humans with humanity.

I dedicate my *Spiritual Songs II: Blessings From A Sacred Soul* to all humans with humanity.

INTRODUCTION

From sacred awakening through the blessed prayers of my inner soul, I was reborn again. I can stand in front of the mirror of life and say today, I am the repented, the redeemed, and the awakened soul, a human within the ocean of life where the lost and stranded roam around waiting to be found. I was the lost and stranded soul who had to stand up and find herself first. I was the traveler who knew the journey of life but goes on. There is no about-turn for this is a one-way highway where the journey begins and ends without our knowledge, yet the traveler's journal we fill up with our own entries.

This traveler's journal I had written within my life thus far came to light as the entries were but reflecting upon the ocean of my life's mirror. As I watched them, I knew I had to accept them first to even move on to the new pages of my traveler's journal. "Accept yourself first," I had told myself, for it is then I can move on to the new beginning. The rebirth of a newly awakened human soul could only be possible when I could see myself and the reflections of my life. Awakened to this new spiritual soul, I had written my first prayer book, *Spiritual Songs: Letters From My Chest.*

I knew my written songs must reach the hands of those whom but seek them. My songs are comfort for the souls of those whom but await their arrival. These sacred songs unite all humans through humanity within one house where life is sacred, and prayers are but sacred songs of the human tears. From the inner soul of a human heart, comes the love for all of humanity.

Today, as I take my second prayer book on her journey through humanity, she takes birth only to hold your hands and comfort you through the obstacles of life. Where you have nothing but tears to guide you, may these songs of prayers be there for you. All throughout my life, I have found comfort within the words of wisdom for all race, color, and religion. My love, my fear, and my blessings came through words of wisdom.

I have written my sacred songs with these sacred words we the humans but have. Where there was no hope, I found hope within the prayers. When I was lost and stranded, I found myself swimming back upon the ark of the prayers. While humans found differences amongst themselves, I found humanity within the prayers I but call songs.

Life is but a day where all begins at dawn and ends as nightfall approaches. Within this day, we the humans must hold on to each other as an oar of life. Where and when one falls, the other becomes the lifesaver by lending a helping hand. My sacred prayers are my helping hands for all of whom but accept them.

I give you my love and blessings through these sacred prayers I call songs. Today, accept these songs as your friend. Be there for all humans across this globe as you too sing these sweet songs in union. Let us the humans not divide amongst ourselves for any reason. Let us be there for all even if our path and homes are but different. For the blessed love of humanity, let us in union sing the sweet songs of harmony. Let us bless all of whom are but different and have different homes.

Let us the different and us the divided, unite for the blessed tune of humanity. The greatest achievement of the humankind is but humanity. To all humans throughout this globe, for the sake of humanity, I give you my blessings through yet another sacred book of prayers.

Her blessed journey begins as you but accept her. Her given name is *Spiritual Songs II: Blessings From A Sacred Soul.*

MESSAGE FROM THE AUTHOR

A sacred soul floating within the ocean of life is awakened for the love of humanity. I had awakened within the pure blessings of my prayer book, *Spiritual Songs: Letters From My Chest.* As I had published my first 100 prayers, I realized prayers for me are like the sweet tune of a blessed song. I wanted to hold on to the sweet and sad tunes of life. My mind, body, and soul wanted to just talk with my Creator. The only way I know how to connect with the invisible force without any religious affiliation is a human calling out to The Creator throughout the journey of life.

How do I ask, seek, and knock upon the invisible door? Where do I find the words, the prayers, and the songs that my heart but asks, seeks, and knocks for? My thoughts had been answered within blessed dreams where I had been blessed to have seen The Holy Archangels. I had been asked if I had written the songs yet. I had seen my written prayers were placed in a bottle and sent to a person who needed a prayer. I have written more about my very personal dreams within my sacred book, *Spiritual Lighthouse: The Dream Diaries Of Ann Marie Ruby.*

I had countless nights thinking *what should I do?* I had countless thoughts of *but what would they say?* Always, I had given greater priority to the harshly spoken mouths of the known and unknown critics of this world. To be a critic or criticize someone is but a word away from just saying nothing or being the voice of appreciation. In reality, however, this world is filled with harsh critics who leave behind tears within a soul they will never even know again. For endless nights, these harsh words are but the painful thorns that hurt so much, yet no words can take over to calm this pain. I had taken prayers to calm my wounded soul and found peace and blessings I had even left behind for the givers of the wound.

I knew I must walk for myself as this journey through my life is my sacred journal left behind for all sacred minds of the future. For the unseen and untouchable pain the sacred soul but feels, I have taken my pen to paper. I have written the blessed songs for my own mind, body, and soul, and for your peaceful mind, body, and soul.

Within one night's dream, I walked out of a cave in which I had taken shelter. I saw Archangel Michael smiling and waiting for me as he said, "So, you are out of the cave. Do you carry the songs with you?" That was a blessed dream as I had within my hands, *Spiritual Songs: Letters From My Chest*, my gift for all.

Life in itself is a blessed miracle where we the travelers have been placed to complete this journey. May you within this life have my *Spiritual Songs* to awaken your inner-self to the peaceful mind, body, and soul of humanity. May your unanswered prayers find themselves upon The Door of Acceptance as you too sing the sweet words of these songs. Today, as you see the reflection of yourself within the rivers of life, may you find these prayers waiting for you within a safely sealed bottle, left there with love and blessings from an unknown friend who had been there in your position, asking, seeking, and knocking for another prayer for my thirsty soul.

May you accept these prayers and awaken your inner-self to humanity for all humans alike. We the humans have only one religion, that is the religion of humankind, the religion of humanity. For all humans with humanity, I now give you my second book of prayers. I call her, *Spiritual Songs II: Blessings From A Sacred Soul.*

TABLE OF CONTENTS

SPIRITUAL SONGS

My Lord, my Creator,

With dawn approaching upon this Earth,

We the creation find the first blessing of the day.

My Lord, my Creator,

May this blessing spread with the wind

Upon us, the creation.

May we find upon our soul,

The first blessed door known as faith.

My Lord, my Creator,

I accept The Omnipotent as my Lord, and all the

Blessings of The Omnipotent as Your love for

This child traveling through this life upon Earth.

My Lord, my Creator,

Forgive this child.

May I never go astray and on this day with dawn,

I repent, redeem, and awaken.

My Lord, my Creator,

May I, Your creation, have upon

My mind, body, and soul, the songs of prayers.

May my recitation be heard

From Heavens above and Earth beneath.

My Lord, my Creator,

May my songs of prayers be my saving grace

From all the obstacles of life.

My Lord, my Creator,

May these songs give all the creation blessed

Health, wealth, and wisdom

To live this life on Earth in peace and harmony.

May these blessed songs of prayers

Bring true soulmates to holy union.

As I sing this prayer of songs,

Accept my prayers my Lord.

Grant me upon this dawn,

All the blessings and protection a child

But needs to live a peaceful life.

My Lord, my Creator,

Accept me for I, with the first blessing of dawn,

Only pray to You with the prayers I but call

SPIRITUAL SONGS.

BLESSINGS FROM A SACRED SOUL

Blessed are but you who have a sacred soul.

Blessed are but you who forgive for love.

Blessed are but you who guide

All the humans without judging.

Blessed are but you the wise, for it is your words

That but guide all to wisdom.

Blessed are but the footsteps of the human who

Travels to only guide all throughout the dark.

Blessed are but you who carry

Within your journey of life,

Love, blessings, and forgiveness.

Blessed is but your journey,

Oh the teacher for you are but our guide.

Blessed are but the students

Who walk behind the truth only to be guided.

On this day, may we the humans but say,

We are all but sacred souls.

Let this be the day,

Let this be the night,

Let this be the time

We all unitedly agree to individually but say,

These are but my,

BLESSINGS FROM

A SACRED SOUL.

THE OMNIPOTENT, THE COMPLETE

My Lord, my Creator,

As dawn breaks through the dark skies,

We the repented, the redeemed, and the awakened

Stand in front of You.

Forgive us my Lord.

Bless us my Lord.

Protect us my Lord

From all sins and obstacles of this world,

Above and beyond.

My Lord, accept our prayers

As we only worship You,

The Complete Oneness,

The Complete Alpha,

The Complete Omega,

THE OMNIPOTENT,

THE COMPLETE.

THE OMNIPRESENCE COMPLETE

Blessed be the sacred prayers

Of the two sacred souls, for within this holy union

Of the mind, the body, and the soul,

Rest the sacred blessings of The Omnipotent.

For within true soulmates,

The sacred prayers are but all found.

For it is the curse of a forced union

That takes all but astray.

Repent, redeem, and know for The Creator,

The Omnipotent's blessings are but found in

The holy union of true soulmates, as all creation

Are but created through this blessed union.

For within this sacred bond of true soulmates

Is but hidden the sacred love of

THE OMNIPRESENCE

COMPLETE.

I TOO AM BUT YOURS

My Lord The Omnipotent,

Dawn is but Your creation.

Darkness is but Your evolution.

The Earth, the mountains,

The plants, the water,

The skies, the stars, the sun, and the moon

Are all but Your existence.

Within all, Your dust is but found.

Within all, life but is.

For within the Earth, the mountains,

The plants, the water,

The skies, the stars, the sun, and the moon,

Life but roams.

Within all creation, love is but found.

My Lord, my Creator,

I, Your creation, only worship You,

For within my existence, my Creator is but found.

Upon me, my Lord, my Creator,

You but laid Your Arms and blessed me with life.

With dawn, I have but awakened and

As nightfall approaches, I shall but lie to sleep.

Throughout this life and eternally,

My Creator shall always but watch over me.

For this my Lord, I but have no fear.

I only have devotion

For wherever my eyes but land as

I know my Lord, my Creator is there,

For all but is Yours my Lord.

This knowledge is but my greatest gift.

From this day, I know

I TOO AM BUT YOURS.

THE HOLY LIGHTS OF HEAVEN

Oh The Holy Lights of Heaven,

Guide me throughout the dark nights.

Hold on to my hands as I walk

Throughout the daylight hours.

My life is a struggle

As I but walk through the obstacles of life.

The Earth, the oceans, the sun, the skies, and

The air, all seem to be polluted with obstacles.

Free me from this punishment of obstacles.

Guide me through this journey.

May I not be buried within the Earth of obstacles.

May I not drown within the oceans of obstacles.

May I not burn myself from these obstacles.

May I not get lost within the skies of obstacles.

May I not stop breathing

Because of these obstacles.

May The Heavenly Lights glow

From within the Earth, the oceans, the sun,

The skies, and the air around me.

Oh Heavenly Lights, turn on your switches

All around me.

Bless me,

Protect me,

Hold on to me

As I find the guidance from Heavens above,

Earth beneath.

Guide me through this journey of life,

Oh The Holy Lights.

May no obstacles but remain upon my path.

May The Holy Lights of Heaven

Guide me to my destiny.

May I eternally be guided by,

THE HOLY LIGHTS

OF HEAVEN.

LET US THE JUDGED NOT BE THE JUDGE

My Lord, my Creator,

Forgive me the sinner.

Guide me the repenter

For I, Your creation, walk

Amongst the sinners, the pious, and the redeemers.

I walk all day and night trying to find

The Path to my Lord, my Creator.

I find humans who but claim to know all,

For they but claim to be the right

As the others are but all wrong.

From the early days of past to the future unknown,

They have committed themselves

In this fight of knowledge.

How could all be right and all be wrong

If the messages are but different

From mouth to mouth?

Oh my Lord, oh my Creator,

Even though everything is unknown,

Mortality looming around is but guaranteed.

They fight against each other,

Proclaiming to be the giver of all the knowledge.

Is it not then they but commit the biggest sin?

Do they not then become The Judge?

Oh my Lord, my Creator,

May I not be amongst them.

May I not be the divider.

May I not do unto them what but has been done

Unto all, by the dividers of this Earth.

May I be able to unite all

Within one prayer, and within one house,

The house known as humanity.

For I know there is but one Judge.

For there is but one Creator.

For there is but one path,

The Path of entry and exit.

Let us the creation unite as humans with humanity.

Let us not commit the gravest sin.

Let us but not judge the other.
LET US THE JUDGED
NOT BE THE JUDGE.

MY DESTINY

My Lord, my Creator, The Omnipotent,

May my destination be

Your will, Your way, and Your words.

May my will not lead me astray.

May my journey through life not end

Within my way.

May my lips not be cursed for my harsh words.

Oh my Lord, oh my Creator, may Your will,

Your way, and Your words be my destiny.

For my Lord's blessings are but hidden

Within The Right Path.

My Lord, my Creator, bless me.

Bless my path, as I choose only Your Guided Path.

Oh my Lord, oh my Creator,

May I not be destined to my destiny.

May my Lord's will, my Lord's way,

And my Lord's words be

MY DESTINY.

BLESSED BE, BLESSED BE, BLESSED BE

Blessed be,

The Lord's mercy is but our saving grace.

Blessed be,

The Lord's mercy is but our only path to salvation.

Blessed be,

The Lord's mercy is but our first and last breath.

Blessed be,

The Lord is but Merciful.

Blessed be,

The Lord but blesses the blessed creation

Each and every day, and may we be but blessed,

With this knowledge of mercy.

BLESSED BE,

BLESSED BE,

BLESSED BE.

MAY I ALWAYS HOLD ON TO MY FAITH

May The Omnipotent's blessings, mercy,

Protection, and forgiveness always be upon us.

May we never go astray,

And always repent, redeem, and awaken

Spiritually and physically.

May we the devotees not carry

Upon our burden of sins,

Jealousy, rage, dissatisfaction,

Or any humanly traits that but take humans astray.

My Lord, hold on to me for,

MAY I ALWAYS HOLD

ON TO MY FAITH.

THE LORD, THE CREATOR

My Lord, my Creator,

Protect Your creation

From the sinful waves of the sinners.

Forgive Your creation, my Lord,

For the sinful traits have drowned all

And converted this world into an ocean of sins.

This world picks up all the sins from the sinners

And but distributes them eternally.

As I walk upon the sinful ocean,

Filled with the sins of the past,

The present, and the future,

May I not become a sinner,

My Lord, my Creator.

May my path be blessed with Your saving grace,

For this is the life vest I but float with,

My Lord, my Creator.

May I not go astray and not drown

Within the ocean of sins,

My Lord, my Creator.

May my repentance and redemption be accepted as

I stand upon Earth only for You,

My Lord, my Creator.

May all obstacles

Known, unknown, seen, or unseen

Be removed from my life,

My Lord, my Creator.

Bless me on this day,

My Lord, my Creator.

Bless me for I am but Your creation,

My Lord, my Creator.

Bless me Your devoted devotee,

For You are

THE LORD,

THE CREATOR.

ACCEPT MY PRAYERS MY LORD

My Lord, my Creator,

Day breaks with hope

As Your sun glows hope within all the houses.

May we have within our home,

Health, wealth, and wisdom.

May all obstacles be removed my Lord.

May we, Your true devotees, have Your blessings,

And may on this day,

Our inner wishes be granted my Lord.

My Lord The Alpha, my Lord The Omega,

Accept our prayers and like the glittering sun,

May hope, love, peace,

And Your blessings be upon us.

My Lord, my Creator,

This devotee shall always stay upon

The Chosen Path of my Lord.

I shall always abide

By the commandments of my Lord.

I shall never go astray

For my love for my Lord is my oath.

Bless my prayers my Lord.

Bless my prayers my Lord.

Bless my prayers my Lord.

Sacred are my prayers I recite

Only for You my Lord.

My Lord, be Merciful.

My Lord, be Merciful.

My Lord, be Merciful.

Accept my prayers my Lord.

Accept my prayers my Lord.

ACCEPT MY PRAYERS

MY LORD.

BLESS THIS CREATION MY LORD

My Lord,

Dawn peeks through the dark, cloudy skies,

Trying to give hope to all of the creation.

I see hope throughout these dark days,

As I know my Lord is there,

Always guiding the lost and stranded,

Always feeding the hungry and needy.

Oh my Lord, may these dark days bring forth

Your blessings upon Your creation.

Oh my Lord, my Creator,

May I the creation always be there

For You my Lord.

As long as there is breath within this creation,

I shall be like the morning glow,

Glowing amongst all of Your creation,

Guiding and protecting Your creation,

As they walk through the dark days.

My Lord, my Creator, may my glow

Catch on amongst Your creation,

And may we the creation glow throughout eternity.

May we be an example

Amongst the lost and stranded

Who but try to find their ways back

To You my Lord.

Oh my Lord, my Creator,

May I be Yours eternally.

On these dark days as I but glow only for You,

BLESS THIS CREATION

MY LORD.

GREATER THAN ALL OBSTACLES COMBINED

My Lord, bless us Your creation.

Obstacles jump in front of us.

From the oceans, from under the Earth,

From the skies, they but appear.

I, Your devotee, fear not,

For I know with all my faith, my pious soul

Shall cross all the obstacles that but appear.

All obstacles combined

Within the oceans, the Earth, and the skies,

Are but nothing for my Lord

The Omnipotent,

The Omniscience

Is

GREATER THAN ALL OBSTACLES COMBINED.

ACCEPT THIS PRAYER OF AN INNOCENT SOUL

My Lord The Alpha, my Lord The Omega,

May The Omnipotent's blessings and protection

Always be upon us the creation.

May we never go astray and always be upon

The Blessed Path of The Omnipotent.

From the first breath to the last,

May the innocence never be lost

From this blessed soul.

May our prayers be accepted,

As a prayer from the innocent soul

Never goes unseen or unheard.

Blessed be, blessed be, blessed be.

My Lord The Alpha, my Lord The Omega,

ACCEPT THIS PRAYER

OF AN INNOCENT SOUL.

MY LORD WITH
THE LANTERN

Let there be light, my Lord,

Within us the humans throughout eternity.

Let the glowing faith of our inner soul

Guide us back to You my Lord.

I but ask, seek, and knock upon

The glowing lights of the night skies,

And the glowing lights beneath the deep oceans,

For they but carry the proof of my Lord.

I watch the lights and follow them

Throughout eternity,

For they but guide all of humankind and

Become the candles of Earth.

Oh my Lord,

I know You but light all the candles of Earth,

From the one and only lantern,

Of The Omniscience.

Oh my Lord,

I know You but call upon all creation

To ask, to seek, and to knock upon

The One and Only Door,

From within where but awaits The Omniscience,

MY LORD WITH

THE LANTERN.

MAY MY MIND, BODY, AND SOUL BE ONLY YOURS

My Lord, may I, Your creation, awaken

Within my mind, body, and soul.

May I not search all over this Earth for repentance,

For repentance is but within my soul, my Lord.

May I never go astray,

And always repent, redeem, and be awakened

From all sins, sinners, evil, or any negativities.

May all the obstacles

Be washed away from my path

Like Your rain washes away

All obstacles on her path.

Oh my Lord, my Creator,

From the mountains to the oceans,

Through each and all of Your creation,

May my lips only praise You and Your words.

My Lord, my Creator,

May my prayers not go lost in the oceans of sins,

But reach Your blessings,

And be accepted and answered by You.

My Lord, bless this soul as I ask, seek, and knock

Only upon Your forgiveness for all of my sins.

Bless me my Lord.

Bless me my Lord.

Bless me my Lord.

My Lord, my Creator,

From dawn through dusk, through dawn,

May I only worship You.

For eternity my Lord,

MAY MY MIND,

BODY, AND SOUL

BE ONLY YOURS.

MAY MY OBSTACLES BE NO MORE

My Lord, my Creator,

Lift me up from the struggles and obstacles of life.

Life is but a house filled with obstacles.

Wherever I stand and as far as my eyes land,

I only find obstacles.

My soul wants to cross the oceans

And climb the invisible mountains

To find You.

Oh my Lord,

How do I but cross the oceans,

To find You?

Oh my Lord,

How do I but climb the invisible mountains,

To find You?

My Lord, answer my prayers

As I only am but a human.

My faith is my only solace my Lord.

My prayers are my only guide my Lord.

My Lord, my Creator, bless me with the miracles,

As You have blessed Your devotees with.

May there be a bridge over the oceans.

May the invisible mountains be no more.

My Lord, may all the obstacles,

Known and unknown to these human eyes,

Be removed.

My Lord, my Creator,

If obstacles are but teachers of life,

I the student, and I the devotee

Have but learned my lessons.

So, for graduation,

With head bowed down in prostration,

Hands in salutation,

I repent, redeem, and awaken.

My Lord, my Creator,

MAY MY OBSTACLES

BE NO MORE.

SACRED SOUL OF THE OMNIPOTENT, THE ALPHA, THE OMEGA

My Lord The Omnipotent,

May my prayers be accepted and granted

As they come from my soul.

May my words, my actions, and my path

Be blessed with Your mercy.

May this life be a sacred spiritual journey filled

With peace and serenity my Lord.

On this journey,

May I only worship You.

May I only be Yours.

May I breathe only for You.

May this devotee's life journey be a sacred grace,

A sacred prayer for peace.

May these hands, feet, eyes,

And all of this mind, body, and soul be Yours,

And only Yours my Lord.

May I the human not go astray, but find You,

Your ways, Your words, and Your wisdom

Throughout this blessed journey of life.

Forgive my sins,

Accept my repentance,

And may I the redeemer be a

SACRED SOUL OF

THE OMNIPOTENT,

THE ALPHA,

THE OMEGA.

THE BLESSED LIGHTS OF HEAVEN

My Lord, high above the Earth,

Heaven but lights up to glorify the Earth,

For it is now time to celebrate.

Celebration of lights begins

With all evil burning down to ashes.

Let there be new beginnings,

And let all obstacles of the yesteryears

Be removed.

May we the blessed, the pious, the sacred creation,

Repent, redeem, and awaken.

May all the troubles of yesteryears

Be a lesson learned and removed.

May the future be blessed

As it begins today my Lord.

On this day, Mother Nature showers

And refreshes herself as she awakens

All devotees of The Lord throughout Earth.

On this day, Heavens above and Earth beneath

Celebrate the victory of good versus evil.

The stars, the oceans, and the mountains

All but celebrate in union,

THE BLESSED LIGHTS

OF HEAVEN.

PEACE, LOVE, AND JOY

My Lord, my Creator,

May I, Your creation, be safe and protected

From all obstacles of life.

May my repentance be accepted.

May I the redeemer be awakened as a pious soul.

Oh my Lord,

Bless this day,

Bless this hour.

My Lord, my Creator,

May this life be filled with

PEACE, LOVE, AND JOY.

MY LORD THE ALPHA, THE OMEGA

My Lord The Omnipotent,

My Lord The Alpha, The Omega,

My Lord, my Creator,

Blessed are Your commands.

Blessed are Your ways.

Blessed are Your words.

Blessed, blessed, blessed are we,

The blessed creation who but know,

The true blessings are but found within,

MY LORD THE ALPHA,

THE OMEGA.

MAY MY FAITH BE MY SAVING GRACE

My Lord, my Creator,

May my prayers reach Your Door.

I have crossed the obstacles, the hardships,

And all the tests life can give a soul my Lord.

In front of me, lies an ocean.

All around me, I have mountains.

Underneath me, the lands fill up with unknown

And unseen hurdles of life

Like quicksand my Lord.

Yet with complete faith, I stand blindfolded

With all of these obstacles.

Guided by my faith, I walk my Lord.

May my faith be The Ark

As I cross over the ocean my Lord.

May my faith be the steps through the mountains

As I walk over the hills of obstacles my Lord.

May my faith be the branch of life holding me

And guiding me through the known, unknown,

Seen, and unseen hurdles of life my Lord.

Save me my Lord.

Protect me my Lord.

Bless me my Lord.

For eternity, I pray only to You,

MAY MY FAITH BE

MY SAVING GRACE.

MY LORD, MY CREATOR THE OMNIPOTENT

My Lord, protect me from

All obstacles, all sins, all insecurities, and all evil.

Oh my Lord, my Creator, grant me

Good health, wealth, and wisdom,

So I may be safe and blessed within this world.

My Lord, may my innocent prayers

From my innocent soul be accepted and blessed.

Oh my Lord, my Creator,

I pray only to You throughout the day

And throughout the night,

For I only worship,

MY LORD, MY CREATOR

THE OMNIPOTENT.

THE HOLY PRAYERS

May the blessings and protection

Of The Omnipotent be upon us

As we repent, redeem, and awaken.

May our heartfelt prayers be our saving grace

Throughout eternity.

May we the saved, the blessed, the redeemed,

Never fall prey to the evil.

May our prayers hold us strong

Throughout all the storms of life.

May all obstacles evaporate

As our prayers become like the ray of the sun.

May we the creation hold on to the only hope

We have throughout eternity, the blessed prayers.

For I know my Lord, my saving grace

For eternity is but,

THE HOLY PRAYERS.

ACCEPT THIS SIN FREE SOUL

My Lord, I, Your creation,

But repent, redeem, and awaken.

May my repentance, redemption, and awakening

Be accepted.

Accept me my Lord.

Accept me my Lord.

Accept me my Lord.

Please accept my repentance, redemption,

And awakening my Lord,

For my soul is but pure and clean.

Sinner I was, pious I am.

With this redemption, may I the pious be free

From all of my committed sins.

Oh my Lord, may I never sin or go astray.

My Lord, accept this sin free soul

As I repent, redeem, and awaken.

Oh my Lord, accept this sin free soul.

Oh my Lord, accept this sin free soul.

Oh my Lord,

ACCEPT THIS

SIN FREE SOUL.

COMMANDMENTS OF MY LORD BE MY DESTINY

My Lord The Omnipotent,

May this day bring forth upon our fate

Blessings, grace, and forgiveness.

May we the devotees not go astray

Or be lost within the sinful oceans.

May our repentance and redemption

Awaken our pure soul.

My Lord, bless us on this day

With health, wealth, and wisdom,

To live a serene, sacred, and peaceful life.

May within this life, we be blessed with

Love, blessings, grace, and may the

COMMANDMENTS OF

MY LORD

BE MY DESTINY.

BLESSED BE THIS LIFE

Just as dawn breaks through the night sky,

May our repentance and redemption also break

Through and reach The Door of Forgiveness.

May we be free from all the sins

Of this mind, body, and soul.

May The Omnipotent's forgiveness, blessings,

And protection always be upon us.

May this dawn bring forth upon our door,

Blessings from Heavens above.

Throughout this day and throughout this night,

We only worship The Omnipotent.

Bless us with the miracles of this world my Lord,

As our inner wishes but come true within this day.

Blessed be this day.

Blessed be this night.

Blessed be, blessed be,

BLESSED BE THIS LIFE.

MY LORD, MY CREATOR, HAVE MERCY

My Lord The Omnipotent,

Protect me from all the adversities of life.

Oh my Lord, protect me from all hidden evil.

Oh my Lord, let The Door of Truth be open

To my mind, body, and soul.

Oh my Lord, The Omnipresence,

May my eyes only see the truth.

Oh my Lord, may my ears only hear

The sweet prayers of Your praise.

Oh my Lord, may my lips only sing the songs of

My Lord The Omniscience.

Oh my Lord, may I, Your creation, awaken

Within complete inner rejuvenation,

Within complete blessings, mercy, and love

Of my Lord The Omnipotent, The Omnipresence,

The Omniscience,

The One and Only Creator of the creation.

My Lord, my Creator, have mercy.

My Lord, my Creator, have mercy.

MY LORD,

MY CREATOR,

HAVE MERCY.

BLESSINGS OF MY LORD, THE OMNIPOTENT

My Lord The Omnipotent,

As the streaming light of hope erupts

Through the lands, the oceans, and the skies,

I awaken from my deep sleep of meditation.

With hands held up high, head bowed down,

I only worship You.

May my repentance and redemption

Cleanse my mind, body, and soul.

Oh my Lord, the miracle of dawn washes away

All the fear as I see the streaming hope

Glow throughout my journey of life.

May I have within this journey Your blessings,

Your forgiveness, and Your grace my Lord.

May the day bring forth miracles

From Heavens above and Earth beneath.

My Lord, may Your Guiding Angels be there

Throughout my life as my saving grace.

Oh my Lord, my Creator,

Throughout the dark nights,

I but hold on to the blessings of hope.

As dawn breaks open,

I but hold on to the miracles of Heavens above.

Throughout the journey of my life,

I the blessed creation but know,

Blessed be my life for I have the

BLESSINGS OF

MY LORD,

THE OMNIPOTENT.

DOOR OF
THE MERCIFUL

Oh my Lord, my Creator,

My Lord The Alpha, The Omega,

My Lord The All-Knowing, The All-Forgiving,

Where do I the helpless, the lost,

The needy but go my Lord?

Why do all these obstacles, these hurdles,

But appear within my life my Lord?

When will all of these physical and

Spiritual obstacles but fade away my Lord?

When and how will this physically and spiritually

Helpless, needy, and lost soul be saved my Lord?

Oh my Lord, my Creator,

Forgive me,

Save me,

Bless me,

For I repent,

For I redeem.

May this repentance and this redemption

Receive Your forgiveness, and

Your blessings my Lord, my Creator.

May this human soul

Find but the sacred blessings,

And the sacred forgiveness of my Lord,

My Creator The Omnipotent.

My Lord The Omnipotent,

May this needy and helpless soul find refuge

Within Your mercy.

May this repented soul find a way out

From all the obstacles my Lord.

Oh my Lord The Omnipotent,

May I the repented, the redeemed creation

Find within my praying soul, Your mercy.

May I find mercy my Lord.

May I find mercy my Lord.

May I find mercy my Lord.

Oh my Lord The Omnipotent,

May I, Your creation,

With complete repentance and

With complete redemption

Find mercy my Lord.

Oh my Lord The Omnipotent,

May these repented and redeemed words

Of prayers but reach Your mercy my Lord.

My Lord The Omnipotent,

On this day, within this sacred blessed prayer,

I the repented and redeemed soul ask of You,

May my prayers but reach the

DOOR OF

THE MERCIFUL.

MY FAITH WITHIN MY LORD THE OMNIPOTENT

My Lord, my Creator, with the first sight of light,

I awaken with hope of a long day.

I end up at sunset and realize but the day has

Left me behind and the darkness awaits in front.

May I, Your devotee, not fear the dark.

May I, Your devotee, not hide within the dark.

May I, Your devotee, be the glowing candle

Amongst the dark.

May I, Your devotee, be there to guide all travelers

Who are but lost for I know after the dark night,

Dawn but appears with blessings, mercy, and hope.

Within my soul, I have but the miracle of eternity,

MY FAITH WITHIN

MY LORD

THE OMNIPOTENT.

THIS DEVOTEE'S PRAYERS BE ACCEPTED AND BE COMPLETE

Oh my Lord The Forgiver,

Oh my Lord The Merciful,

Forgive this devotee.

This life has given hurdles

And obstacles upon my path.

This life has brought upon my path,

Fear and destruction.

Protect me my Lord.

Show me a way out my Lord,

As I wait for The Door of Acceptance.

Oh my Lord, my Creator,

This creation waits for The Door of Repentance,

The Door of Forgiveness,

And The Door of Acceptance to open.

Take me up within Your protection my Lord.

My Lord, save me from all the obstacles,

And the hurdles beyond any human control.

Show me The Door of Acceptance

As I travel through This Door of Life.

My Lord, my Creator,

I am Your creation, alone and lost,

Floating amongst all different paths

Created by Your creation.

I, Your creation, only ask, seek, and knock

For You, Your Blessed Path, Your blessed words,

And Your blessed messages.

May my path be Your Given Path

And may my mind, body, and soul

Only have prayers of guidance,

Guiding me throughout eternity.

My Lord, my Creator,

On this day, may I, Your creation,

Have within my path,

Your acceptance of this Earthy devotee.

May I have no fear and may all of my hurdles

And obstacles be removed as I walk within

The Blessed Path of The Omnipotent,

From Heavens above throughout Earth beneath.

May on this day,

THIS DEVOTEE'S

PRAYERS BE ACCEPTED

AND BE COMPLETE.

A NEW DAY

My Lord, as the world brings upon us

Yet another day,

I know I must pray and give my grace

For this bright new day.

My Lord, may this new day remove

All of the obstacles of yesterday.

May this day be the new birth of hope

And blessings upon the lives of all whom

But raise their hands up in a prayer.

May the prayers of sacred souls reach Your Door,

As I ask, seek, and knock for all only to You,

My Lord, my Creator.

Accept my prayers my Lord and bless me today

As this is a new beginning

For this is but,

A NEW DAY.

BLESSED BE THE DAWN THAT BRINGS UPON US THE DAY

Oh my Lord The Omnipotent,

May this dawn bring forth blessings,

Mercy, and forgiveness upon me.

May this dawn give me a blessed day.

May this day be but according to Your will.

May I, Your creation, not fall prey to

My own laziness or physical pain.

May no obstacles from this world or beyond

But fall upon me my Lord,

For I have so much to accomplish on this day.

May I, Your devotee, be able

And may Your blessings be upon me.

Oh my Lord, let all physical illnesses be removed

As Mother Earth is but the healer, the purifier,

And I am her child.

My home is but upon her chest

As I awaken upon this day.

Oh my Lord, let me gather all that I must gather

On this day before nightfall appears

Upon this Earth.

Oh my Lord, may all my efforts of this day

Save me and brighten my home.

May my family be safe throughout the nightfall

As we hold on to the candles of hope,

Throughout the dark nights.

Oh my Lord, bless us on this day

As we awaken only for You.

Blessed be the day,

We the devotees must not take in vain.

We must pray for we are but Your creation,

Awakened and blessed to have this day.

BLESSED BE THE DAWN

THAT BRINGS UPON US

THE DAY.

THE MERCIFUL, BLESSED BE, BLESSED BE, BLESSED BE

My Lord The Merciful,

Blessed be.

All the blessings, all the mercy is but Your giving,

Blessed be.

As this dawn takes us through this blessed day,

Blessed be.

Throughout this day, the blessings given to us are

But Your mercy, oh my Lord The Merciful,

Blessed be.

With sundown, nightfall but approaches

Upon our path.

May we be the candles of hope

For all Your creation, oh my Lord The Merciful,

Blessed be.

Oh my Lord, may this nightfall take us to dawn

With honor, dignity, and courage,

Oh my Lord The Merciful,

Blessed be.

Oh my Lord, my Creator,

Hold on to my hands

Throughout this journey of my life.

From dawn through dusk through dawn,

May I always be only Yours

As You are but my Lord, my Creator,

THE MERCIFUL,

BLESSED BE,

BLESSED BE,

BLESSED BE.

SAVED BY THE GRACE OF MY LORD THE OMNIPOTENT

My Lord, forgive, forgive, forgive.

Let the sins of this Earth not take over

My mind, body, and soul.

My Lord, let this unknown and unseen

Ocean of sins not drown me.

Oh my Lord, all around me

I only see the overflowing sins.

My Lord, I search for the lifesavers.

My Lord, I search for the ray of hope

To find my way out of this sinful ocean.

My Lord, cold, tired, and frail,

I float all alone, searching for hope.

Bless me my Lord.

Save me my Lord.

May this ocean of sins not drown me my Lord.

May the ocean of sinners

Not carry me away from You my Lord.

May the spiritual lighthouse

Show me the candles of hope my Lord.

May I have upon my lips

The spiritual songs my Lord.

May I the repented and the redeemed find myself

Upon the spiritual ark my Lord.

May I the repented and the redeemed be

SAVED BY THE GRACE

OF MY LORD

THE OMNIPOTENT.

THE FINAL JUDGE

My Lord, my Creator,

Forgive this mind, this body, and this soul.

Within this Earth, this universe,

And all of the existence,

Sins but have risen from Earth beneath

To the skies above.

Within dawn, the blessed prayers but get lost

And the sounds of sins but gather

Within the inner and outer walls

Of this Earth my Lord.

At dusk as all Your creation,

The birds, the fish, the animals

Look for shelter from the unknown dark,

Your creation, we the humans, go astray

Within the nightly sins.

Oh my Lord, my Creator,

Forgive this sinful mind, body, and soul

As I rise above and beyond all the sins

Of Heavens above and Earth beneath.

My Lord, my Creator,

I carry repentance within my soul.

My body but rises within redemption.

My mind but awakens

Within the blessings and love of my Lord.

I pray as I, Your creation,

Repent, redeem, and awaken for You,

Oh my Lord, my Creator,

The Acceptor of the repented soul,

The Receiver of the redeemers,

The Forgiving,

The Merciful,

THE FINAL JUDGE.

BLESS THIS PRAYER MY LORD

My Lord The Omnipotent,

Bless me, protect me, and keep me safe

From all adversities of life.

My Lord,

Bless me with good health, wealth, and wisdom.

My Lord,

Accept my repentance and redemption

As I awaken sin free, pure, and clean,

Only for the love of my Lord, The Omnipotent.

My Lord,

May I not go astray

And not fall prey to the beast and his ways.

My Lord,

May I always have Your guidance

Throughout eternity.

May this life be only for You my Lord

And may all my efforts be blessed and successful

As I only worship You.

May my prayers reach Your Door from dawn

Through dusk through dawn.

May my lips only be blessed

With blessed words of wisdom,

And may my mind, body, and soul be

In devotion of my Lord The Omnipotent.

Bless this day my Lord.

Bless this soul my Lord.

BLESS THIS PRAYER

MY LORD.

SOULMATES THROUGHOUT ETERNITY

My Lord The Omniscience,

Blessed be the repentance and redemption

Of true soulmates.

From Your blessings, they but unite.

Through Your blessings,

They but awaken only for You.

Bless us my Lord.

Accept the true prayers of pure souls.

Allow true soulmates to unite

And be blessed with this sacred journey

Of soulmates finding each other and uniting.

Bless us my Lord.

Bless this home, bless this land,

And bless this union of true soulmates.

Bless us my Lord, for we the united

Only seek Your blessings.

We pray only to You my Lord The Omnipresence.

Bless our prayers, accept our prayers,

And allow us to be free from all obstacles,

And be with our soulmates in union,

Soul to soul,

Mind to mind,

Body to body.

As one only for You my Lord,

We are but Your created, Your blessed

SOULMATES

THROUGHOUT

ETERNITY.

MY CREATOR, THE OMNIPOTENT

My Lord, protect us from all miseries of life.

May all sufferings be removed from our life.

May we not go astray.

May we have repentance and redemption

Upon our mind, body, and soul.

May we call upon You my Lord The Omnipotent

Throughout eternity and not just when needed,

For I know my Lord's love

For all creation is limitless.

My love for my Lord

Is but my entire life and beyond.

May all creation be blessed

And have their love for The Omnipotent.

It is then, we shall never sin or go astray,

For our love for our Creator

And our Creator's love for us.

Blessed be the blessed prayers.

Blessed be The Door of Repentance.

Blessed be my Lord is always there

And I shall always be there

For my Lord,

MY CREATOR,

THE OMNIPOTENT.

BLESSINGS, MERCY, AND FORGIVENESS

Oh my Lord, my Creator,

Hands up in salutation,

Head bowed down in prostration,

I welcome this dawn as blessings

From Heavens above.

With the arrival of dawn,

I know I have yet another day to repent, redeem,

And do good unto all the creation of my Lord.

My life is blessed as I have yet another day

To live my life in accordance within

The commandments of my Lord, my Creator.

Throughout the evening, I shall light up all

The candles along The Path of my Lord,

So all of the creation may find their way back to

The House of my Lord, my Creator.

As nightfall but approaches, I shall take guidance
From the stars above to guide myself
And all of whom need a guide to walk them
Through the dark nights of their lives.
My Lord, my Creator, bless this mind, body,
And soul as this creation is but
On a journey through life.
Upon this journey, may I, Your creation, not
Be lost and stranded within the sinful ocean of life.
May I, Your creation, awaken upon Your Ark,
Sin free, pure, and clean.
My Lord, my Creator,
As dawn but converts to day,
And day but converts to evening, and
All but become dark as we enter the dark nights,
May I, Your creation, always have Your guidance.
May I have throughout this journey of life,
My Lord, my Creator, The Omnipotent's
BLESSINGS, MERCY,
AND FORGIVENESS.

MY LORD, SEND YOUR SAVING GRACE

As obstacles but corner me from all around,

This devotee stands tall with hands in salutation,

Mind, body, and soul in devotion.

I recite the prayers for my Lord

With complete faith,

For I know a prayer recited from the pure soul

Never goes unheard by Heavens above

And Earth beneath.

Blessed be the power of a prayer,

As all obstacles crumble to ashes

And become dust to dust.

The power of this human mind, body, and soul is

Within the sacred prayers recited by the lips,

Heard from Earth beneath to The Heavens above.

My Lord, my Creator,

From The Blessed Heavens above to

Your Earth beneath,

I ask You to protect me, save me,

And spread the blessings of protection upon me,

As I walk through this life of obstacles.

May these blessed blessings be my shawl

Of protection throughout eternity.

My Lord, my Creator,

As I hold on to the blessed blessings of my shawl

Of prayers, may The Blessed Angels hold on to me

As I walk through the oceans, the mountains,

And the Earth of obstacles.

May I, Your devotee, always be blessed

As within my soul, I carry the sacred blessings of

My Lord, my Creator.

I carry upon my lips,

The blessed prayers of protection.

My Lord protect, my Lord save,

MY LORD, SEND YOUR

SAVING GRACE.

THE OMNIPOTENT'S BLESSINGS

My Lord, may this dawn break

With blessings, mercy, and protection

Upon our path.

My Lord, my Creator,

Today, I awaken as my mind, body, and soul

Awaken sin free, pure, and clean.

Within my soul, I have repentance and redemption.

Within my lips, I recite the blessed prayers,

So I never go astray.

My Lord, my Creator,

May this day bring forth upon my life journey,

The blessings so I can earn Your mercy.

May I have this day to be

Your pure and clean devotee.

As nightfall approaches, may I, Your repented,

Redeemed, and pure devotee,

Not fear the darkness but glow from within

As I carry Your blessings, mercy, and forgiveness

Throughout eternity.

As I awaken spiritually for You,

My Lord, my Creator,

I but fear not anything,

For I have my Lord, my Creator,

THE OMNIPOTENT'S

BLESSINGS.

ACCEPTANCE OF MY LORD, MY CREATOR

My Lord, my Creator,

Sin is but a deadly disease

That has no symptoms or side effects.

Oh my Lord, my Creator,

This invisible force but robs

The mind, body, and soul.

May we the humans hold on to

The blessings of The Omnipotent

And not go astray.

May we not fall prey to the sins of this world.

My Lord, may these deadly sins not drown us

Within the sinful ocean of eternity.

My Lord, may we not fall prey to the sins

Of our own temptations.

My Lord, accept our repentance,

Accept our redemption,

And bless us throughout eternity,

As we the repented, the redeemed,

Awaken sin free, pure, and clean.

Bless us my Lord.

Accept this prayer my Lord,

For I only want the mercy, blessings, and

ACCEPTANCE OF

MY LORD, MY CREATOR.

BLESSED PRAYERS ARE BUT MY SAVING GRACE

My Lord, my Creator,

Let there be light.

Let there be freedom.

Let there be a way out for me.

Let these worldly obstacles not drown this soul.

Let all of these hurdles I face not wipe me out.

My Lord, my Creator,

May I stand strong amongst

All the windstorms of life.

May my faith keep me afloat

Even within the sinful oceans.

My Lord, my Creator,

Let this prayer be my saving grace.

May I be able to hold on to the hands

Of this blessed prayer and be free from all hurdles,

All obstacles, and all adversities of life.

May I find myself within Your grace

As I wash myself within this prayer.

May my mind, body, and soul be immersed

Within this blessed prayer.

May this immersion set me free

From all the obstacles of life.

May there be light,

As I recite this prayer from within my soul.

May there be no remaining hurdles

And may I be free from all obstacles of life.

My Lord, my Creator,

As I but hold on to the hands of this prayer,

I know I shall find my way out from all

The worldly hurdles life but brings upon me.

My Lord, my Creator,

I know when even all seem hopeless

And nothing is but found,

It is then, the

BLESSED PRAYERS ARE

BUT MY SAVING GRACE.

MY COMPLETE FAITH WITHIN MY LORD THE OMNIPOTENT

Obstacles but come upon me without any notice.

They test my faith, my honor, and my patience.

I stand alone, yet I stand steadfast and strong as

I have within my mind, body, and soul,

Faith, honor, and patience.

Within my mind, body, and soul, I have

My Lord, my Creator's blessings and guidance.

I carry upon my soul,

Repentance and forgiveness,

For I know the unjust humans are but

The lost and the stranded who have

Within themselves, false comforts of the day

And false promises of the night.

My Lord, my Creator,

May I, Your creation, not go astray

Within this sinful ocean of life.

May I not be the judge of others, but

May I always hold on to

The hands of faith, honor, and patience.

The false comforts of the day,

Or the false promises of the dark night

Cannot touch me for I have,

MY COMPLETE FAITH

WITHIN MY LORD

THE OMNIPOTENT.

SIN FREE, PURE, AND CLEAN

Blessed be the dawn

That awakens a sin free soul.

Blessed be the pure soul

That but repents from within and awakens sin free.

Blessed be the prayers of a sin free soul.

Blessed be the mind, body, and soul,

That but repent, redeem, and awaken from within.

Oh my Lord, my Creator, bless this soul as

I repent, redeem, and awaken sin free

From all the sins of this world.

May I not go astray and fall prey

To the sins and sinners of this world.

My Lord, may I, Your creation, awaken sin free

As dawn breaks through within my life.

May my life journey be only for You,

My Lord, my Creator.

May this sacred journey be blessed

As I awaken

SIN FREE,

PURE, AND CLEAN.

FOREVER, I ONLY WORSHIP THE OMNIPOTENT COMPLETE

This devoted devotee but has,

Awakened from within only for the love of

My Lord, my Creator.

Oh my Lord,

I have but devoted my entire eternity for You,

To You, as all my devotion is but my love

For my Lord, my Creator.

May my mind, body, and soul be united

Within the truth of eternity.

May I stand above the sins of this world

And beneath the protection of Heavens above.

May my blessings be Your mercy

And acceptance of this mind, body, and soul,

Oh my Lord, my Creator.

Even when this world is no more,

And all but comes to an end,

Even then, may my lips utter the blessed prayers

For my Lord, my Creator.

Through the end, may my hands be in salutation.

When the Apocalypse but arrives

Upon us the humans, may I, Your creation, not be

Distracted from my prayers even then.

May this devotee be in devotion for eternity.

FOREVER,

I ONLY WORSHIP

THE OMNIPOTENT

COMPLETE.

ACCORDANCE OF MY LORD THE OMNIPOTENT

My Lord, life is but complete within

Your mercy, forgiveness, and blessings.

Life begins within Your Hands

And ends but within Your Hands.

Why my Lord, am I left alone

Throughout this journey of my life?

My Lord, obstacles but appear all around me.

Sins and sinners float within dishonesty

All around me my Lord.

May I find my way out of

These life given obstacles my Lord.

May all sins and sinners disappear

As I repent and redeem.

May all obstacles disappear as

I hold on to the blessed prayers for my Lord.

May my lips be blessed within these prayers.

May my mind, body, and soul awaken

With complete devotion and

May my soul always be in complete prostration

Toward my Lord, my Creator.

May my life be complete as

I live my life within the

ACCORDANCE OF

MY LORD

THE OMNIPOTENT.

BLESSED CHILDREN OF GOD

Lost and stranded,

Alone in the ocean of sins I find myself,

My Lord, my Creator.

All around me, obstacles and hurdles appear

Drowning me my Lord.

Bless this child my Lord.

May I throughout all of these obstacles have

Your blessings, Your mercy, and

Your forgiveness my Lord.

Throughout the ocean of sins, I will float sin free

With the blessed life jacket filled

With blessings of my Lord.

Throughout all the dark obstacles of life,

I will hold on to the blessed torches of my Lord.

Throughout my life, may I, Your devotee,

Hold on to the blessed blessings of

My Lord, my Creator,

For I know within this life,

All this child shall ever ask for is but

Your blessings my Lord,

For I am but Your child,

For we are all but the

BLESSED CHILDREN

OF GOD.

ANSWERED BY MY LORD THE OMNIPRESENCE

Oh The Remover of all obstacles and calamities,

I ask of You on this day, please remove all the

Obstacles and calamities from my life.

My Lord, may this blessed day

Bring forth upon my life all the openings

To The Doors of Protection and Blessings.

Against all the odds and against

All the worldly beliefs, I know my Lord

The Omnipresence is always watching over me.

With prayers upon my lips, and

My inner soul, the complete beholder of my faith,

I know I shall always hold on to my Lord,

For I know my Lord, even throughout

All the obstacles and calamities of life, I shall walk

Only for You, my Lord The Omnipresence.

For all above and all beneath

The Heavens and the Earth,

I only call upon You my Lord The Omnipresence.

For I know even when all is dark,

And nothing is left, my life is but completely full

As I know You are always present

Throughout eternity.

My Lord, on this day I ask of You,

Please hold on to this devoted devotee as I ask You

To carry me to my destination as this devoted soul

Has no other way but You, my Lord.

May I be at the destination where life shall bring

The answers to my blessed sacred prayers.

May This Blessed Door be open now my Lord.

May my prayers reach Your Door.

May my prayers be accepted.

May my prayers be

ANSWERED BY,

MY LORD

THE OMNIPRESENCE.

COMPLETE HOPE AND COMPLETE FAITH

Blessed be hope and blessed be faith.

Blessed be the souls

Who carry within themselves hope and faith.

For where there is hope, there is my Lord.

For where there is faith, there is my Lord.

For where there is life, there is hope,

And where there is belief, there is faith.

For hope and faith in union

Complete this life's journey.

Where and when there is nothing,

And all seem hopeless,

It is then we the humans

Must call upon our hope and faith,

For within this powerful mystery,

God is but found.

God The Omnipotent,

God The Omnipresence

But is found where and when there is,

COMPLETE HOPE AND

COMPLETE FAITH.

THROUGHOUT ETERNITY

My Lord is but my saving grace.

My Lord is but my faith throughout eternity.

My Lord is but the only hope I have, I hold,

And I shall belong to throughout eternity.

As the skies turn dark

From the storm brewing above the Earth,

As the Earth cracks beneath our feet,

As the oceans flood all over the lands,

Destroying homes and lives,

Even then I hold on to my faith

As the End of Time but brews

All around the Earth.

My Lord, my Creator,

This mind, body, and soul have been in devotion

For You throughout eternity.

Even when all but had begun, I was in devotion,

And when all but shall end, I, Your devotee,

Will be in complete devotion for

My Lord, my Creator.

Within my Lord is but all of my faith.

Within my Lord, all humans are but one

As we the humans are all but the creation

Of This One Creator.

Oh my Lord, I ask of You on this day,

Even when all that is but ends,

Even when nothing is but left,

Even then, may this devotee's

Eternal love for my Lord, exist

THROUGHOUT

ETERNITY.

FIRST BLESSINGS OF DAWN

Dawn peeks through

And spreads the glimmer of hope

Through the open windows

Of all whom but seek.

I accept Your blessings of dawn my Lord

For I know dawn is but

My Lord's first gift of the day

For the awakened and devoted souls.

This day is but the blessed answer

To the seekers of the prayers.

May we the seekers open the doors and windows

Of our mind, body, and soul,

And accept all the blessings of this glorious day.

My Lord, may this day

End the hurdles of the dark night.

May they disappear

Through the first blessings of dawn.

My Lord, may I, Your creation, awaken

Sin free, pure, and clean,

As I accept the sacred blessings of this day.

Blessed be the day.

Blessed be the blessings of my Lord.

Blessed be the

FIRST BLESSINGS

OF DAWN.

SACRED BLESSINGS AND LOVE OF THE OMNIPRESENCE

Blessed be the journey of a repented soul.

Throughout life, sins float all around

As this soul but repents, redeems, and awakens

For the love of truth, justice, and honor.

This soul seeks only The Right Path.

This soul walks reciting the blessed sacred prayers,

To be guided by,

To be protected by,

To be saved by.

This soul holds on to the only path

Seen by the human eyes, The Right Path.

Blessed be this human soul but carries

Throughout the journey of life, humanity.

Blessed be the prayers of a righteous soul.

Bless this soul on this day my Lord.

Never shall this soul but go astray,

Or fall prey to the beast, or his ways.

Never again shall wrong be done by this soul

For within this soul is but the

SACRED BLESSINGS

AND LOVE OF

THE OMNIPRESENCE.

THE JUDGMENT DAY

My Lord, Your sun breaks through

After the dark night's struggle

To bring daylight within our lives.

This devotee salutes and prostrates only to You

Throughout the night and throughout the day.

May I be covered within blessings

Throughout the cold shivering nights

And not by the sins of the humans.

Throughout the day,

May Your sun hold on to me.

May I be there awakened within the

Blessings my Lord but bestows upon me

And not within the sins of the human mind.

My Lord, may my life be an example

Of a true devotee who stands alone

If that is the truthful way,

But shall stand up for You my Lord, my Creator.

May the world not take me astray,

But may I take upon my mind, body, and soul,

The guidance of The Omnipotent, The

Omnipresence, The Omniscience.

My Lord The Alpha, my Lord The Omega,

May I be blessed amongst all by You on

THE JUDGMENT DAY.

HOUSE OF THE LORD, THE CREATOR

As the sun but sets after the day ends,

All but evolve within darkness.

Throughout my nights and throughout my days,

May I be within the protection and blessings

Of my Lord, my Creator.

Within the dark nights,

May I have the blessed candles of my Lord.

Throughout the daylight hours,

May I be within The Blessed Path

Of my Lord, my Creator.

Throughout the journey of my life,

May I not go astray or drown

Within the sinful oceans.

Blessed be the dark nights,

For then I shall but be

A candle glowing within the darkness,

To guide myself and all of whom

But need guidance to The House of my Lord.

Blessed be the daylight hours

For then I shall ask, seek, and knock,

On all doors of whom have but gone astray

To come back to The House of

My Lord, my Creator.

Eternally grateful my mind, body, and soul are,

For I have but found

The Door to The

HOUSE OF THE LORD,

THE CREATOR.

BELOVED CREATOR, THE ALPHA, THE OMEGA

Life blesses all at birth.

Life glows within all throughout eternity,

For I know my Lord, this life was created

Before my entry onto Earth.

This life was, is, and shall always be blessed,

As it is but the complete blessing of

My Lord, my Creator.

Blessed is but the birth of all souls as the soul is

But always complete within the complete love

And devotion of The Creator.

My Lord, my Creator but loves this creation

For I was but created by my

BELOVED CREATOR,

THE ALPHA,

THE OMEGA.

BLESSED HANDS OF THE OMNIPOTENT

My Lord The Alpha, The Omega,

Within Your Hands, all but began.

Within Your Hands, all but shall end.

My Lord, my Creator, within You, all life but is.

For You, I but am.

Within Your command, my destiny but is.

For You, I but exist and for You, I shall but live.

Within the commandments of my Lord,

I am but blessed.

Within the guidance of my Lord,

I am but complete for this life is but the

Sacred blessing of my Lord, my Creator.

For even when all but ends,

This creation is but immortal within the

BLESSED HANDS OF

THE OMNIPOTENT.

MY LORD THE OMNIPOTENT, IS BUT MY SALVATION

Ask, seek, and knock, my Lord but says,

Yet we the humans

Never listen, and

Never see,

The questions and answers my Lord but provides.

Oh my Lord, may I not fall prey to the sins

Of my own life's journey.

May I not be a burden

Upon my own journey through life.

May my mind, body, and soul not go astray

To this worldly view of salvation.

May my salvation be

Through the blessed prayers for my Lord.

May my salvation be

Through the blessed words of my Lord.

May my salvation be

Through the commandments of my Lord.

May my salvation be

Through my repentance, redemption and

Awakening bath, oh my Lord,

For I know upon The Blessed Sacred Hands of

MY LORD

THE OMNIPOTENT,

IS BUT MY SALVATION.

SUNG THROUGHOUT ETERNITY

My Lord, my Creator,

Blessed be the dawn

That breaks through all of the obstacles of life.

Blessed be the sun

That evaporates all of the hurdles of life.

Blessed be this life

That shines after all of the obstacles.

Blessed be my Lord The Omnipresence,

Shining throughout the day and night,

Guiding all creation throughout eternity.

Blessed be this devotee's prayers

Be heard throughout eternity as

The love for my Lord shall be immortally

SUNG THROUGHOUT

ETERNITY.

UPON
THE OMNIPOTENT

Blessed be this day.

Blessed be the prayers recited

By a devotee on this day.

My Lord, bless this mind, body, and soul,

As this day brings forth all the sacred blessings

From Heavens above and Earth beneath.

Bless this creation my Lord, as I awaken sin free,

Pure, and clean, within the bath of repentance.

My Lord, my Earthly body in devotion,

My soul always in prostration,

As for all my blessings,

I only ask, seek, and knock,

UPON

THE OMNIPOTENT.

THE ARK OF MY LORD IS BUT FOUND

Dark skies evolve all around the ocean,

Where lightning is the only hope of light, yet the

Sound frightens all above and beyond, my Lord.

All humans floating within this sinful ocean of sins

Are but oblivious to the sinful actions

Of their lives my Lord.

Right and wrong have no space as all is but

Forceful voices and will of their might my Lord.

May I, Your devotee, not drown

Amongst all of this my Lord.

May my faith be my saving grace my Lord.

May my faith be my wisdom of life my Lord.

May my faith be my honor my Lord.

May my faith lead me

To The Door of Repentance my Lord,

For within This Door is but

The Blessed Ark of my Lord.

Within This Ark, all are but saved and

All are but free from all the obstacles of life,

For I know within each repented, redeemed,

And awakened soul,

THE ARK OF MY LORD

IS BUT FOUND.

BLESSED BE MY LOVE FOR MY CREATOR

Blessed be the love of my Lord for all creation.

Blessed be this true love

From Heavens above and Earth beneath,

For this pure love keeps all in harmony.

Blessed be the love of a mother for her child.

Blessed be the sacred blessings of all strangers

Who but become Angels,

For this powerful feeling of true love.

Blessed be the creation

Who but repents, redeems, and awakens for love.

For this sacred bond of love,

I shall never go astray.

BLESSED BE MY LOVE

FOR MY CREATOR.

THE ALPHA, THE OMEGA

Blessed be the day the devotee but awakens.

Blessed be the prayers of a devoted devotee,

For within the mind, body, and soul

Is but all the love of a devotee for The Creator.

Blessed be the devotion.

Blessed be the prostration.

Blessed be the hands of the blessed devotee,

Immersed in complete devotion.

Blessed be the complete love of the devotee

For The Creator, The Omnipotent,

THE ALPHA,

THE OMEGA.

GUIDE ALL THROUGHOUT ETERNITY

Will power and determination I have

For You my Lord, my Creator.

Never shall I but sin.

Never shall I but go astray.

Never shall I but go against the commandments

Of my Lord, my Creator.

Never shall this mind, body, or soul

But swim into the sinful oceans,

For I shall hold on to my ark of faith

And float even within the sinful oceans.

The sinful waters will not touch me,

Nor shall they drown me for my love for my Lord

Is but my saving grace.

As I float upon this Earth,

My Lord's musical words, and

My Lord's beloved

Musical tunes but shall

GUIDE ALL

THROUGHOUT ETERNITY.

FROM THE BEHOLDER TO THE BELOVED

The blessed music of eternal love

But plays throughout time.

Throughout the air,

Throughout the pouring rain,

Throughout the heated sun,

This musical blessing but awakens all sacred souls.

The trees but dance in glory.

The birds but sing throughout time.

The animals hide out of fear, but come out as

They too love this musical tune.

The Earth but awakens with joy.

The sun and moon but dance within the skies.

All of this universe is but awakened,

As the stars dance throughout the night skies,

For they know what the humans know of not.

The musical notes that but unite all creation

With The Creator

Are but the inner songs of a prayer,

FROM THE BEHOLDER

TO THE BELOVED.

THE LOVE AND GRACE OF MY LORD THE OMNIPOTENT

Blessed be, the love of my Lord

Is but my saving grace.

Blessed be, the prayers of this soul

Are but my awakening path.

Blessed be, the repentance for it is then

The repented soul has but found The Right Path.

Blessed be, The Path is there for us to find

And be guided by.

Blessed be, the travelers taking

A journey through life.

Blessed be, the life journey of the traveler

Is but eternal through

THE LOVE AND GRACE

OF MY LORD

THE OMNIPOTENT.

BLESSINGS, MERCY, AND PROTECTION OF MY LORD THE OMNIPOTENT

Oh my Lord, let there be protection within my life

From all hurdles approaching my way.

Oh my Lord, let there be healing within my mind,

Body, and soul from all known and unknown

Attacks coming with or without any warning.

Oh my Lord, let all known and unknown obstacles

Taking birth within my path of life

Be dissolved into nothingness.

Oh my Lord, let this creation traveling through this

Journey of life be blessed as I carry the

BLESSINGS, MERCY,

AND PROTECTION,

OF MY LORD

THE OMNIPOTENT.

120

BATH OF REPENTANCE

Oh my Lord, my Creator,

Life is but Your complete blessing

As life begins within Your Hands

And but ends within Your Hands.

All I have are my repentance, my redemption, and

The blessings from my Lord, my Creator for this is

All I need to travel through this journey of life.

May I, Your creation, not go astray.

May I, Your creation, not fall prey

To the sins of this life.

May my mind and body not sin, and drown

My soul which was but created pure and clean.

My Lord, my Creator, may my life on this Earth

Be a blessed bath through

My repentance, redemption, and awakening.

My Lord, my Creator, may my mind, body,

And soul in union, awaken sin free as I take the

BATH OF REPENTANCE.

THE WILL OF MY LORD, THE OMNIPOTENT

I accept my Lord, The Omnipotent.

I accept my Lord, The Omniscience.

I accept The Complete Lord, The Divine Creator,

The Alpha, The Omega

As my only Lord, my Creator.

For I know within this acceptance,

I have the complete divine truth.

The complete reason of my existence is but,

THE WILL OF MY LORD,

THE OMNIPOTENT.

THE HOPE FOR ALL HUMANITY

Blessed be the repentance of a repented soul.

Lost are the repeated sinners

Who have but gone astray,

My Lord, my Creator,

For they have taken for granted

The love, the blessings, and the mercy of

The Forgiving Lord, The Omnipotent.

My Lord, I know there are but

Your Doors to Heavens above

And The Doors to the burning Hell below.

May Your judgment be our last hope,

For I know the human sinners would even curse

Themselves if they had not known

They are but judging themselves.

Oh my Lord,

Blessed be The Judge of The Judgment Day,

For within The Hands of The Final Judge rests,

THE HOPE FOR
ALL HUMANITY.

ETERNAL LOVE FOR MY LORD THE OMNIPOTENT

Blessed be the dawn after darkness but evaporates.

Blessed be the prayers of a repented soul.

Blessed be the soul which has awakened for

The love of The Omnipotent.

Blessed be the love that unites the creation

With The Creator.

For I know my Lord,

Within this world,

All but ends as all humans

Complete their journey through life.

All that survive throughout eternity

Are but my love for my Lord,

And my Lord's love for me,

Which keep me safe throughout eternity.

Oh my Lord, this is my eternal truth,

For this truth is but blessed

Within my mind, body, and soul.

This is but my

ETERNAL LOVE

FOR MY LORD

THE OMNIPOTENT.

PHYSICAL AND EMOTIONAL PAIN

Oh my Lord The Healer,

My Lord The Giver and The Remover

Of all physical and emotional pain,

Today on this Earth, Your creation,

Your devoted humans are in pain my Lord.

Bless us with the mercy of healing my Lord.

Bless this devotee and may

All physical and emotional pain be removed.

Oh The Merciful,

Oh The Remover of all obstacles,

Oh The Healer,

Blessed be this day and blessed be this night,

As my Lord The Omnipotent but grants

The wishes of this repented soul.

Bless this time and bless this hour my Lord,

As I, Your devotee, raise my hands only to You.

Forgive me for all the known and unknowns sins

Committed by this repented mind, body, and soul.

Oh my Lord, on this day,

Hear my heartfelt prayer.

Heal this mind, body, and soul my Lord

From all the known and unknown,

PHYSICAL AND

EMOTIONAL PAIN.

ETERNALLY YOURS, THIS SOULMATE'S HEART BUT BEATS

From mind to mind,

Body to body,

Soul to soul,

My Lord but creates true love.

Within the union of two souls,

My Lord's blessings are but found.

From Heavens above and Earth beneath,

My Lord but creates one for another.

The Angels above and beyond

Rejoice as true soulmates but unite.

My Lord, my Creator,

On this day, grant me but one prayer

As I but ask, seek, and knock upon Your Door.

May my mind, body, and soul,

Eternally belong only to my soulmate.

Throughout eternity,

May my soulmate see, hear, and know

ETERNALLY YOURS,

THIS SOULMATE'S

HEART BUT BEATS.

THE BELOVED CREATION OF THE BELOVED LORD

My Lord The Omnipotent, The Omnipresence,

Bless Your children my Lord.

Bless our ways my Lord,

For we walk only on Your Path.

Bless our speech my Lord,

For we only speak of Your words.

Bless our minds my Lord,

For we seek the knowledge of Your truth.

Bless our lips my Lord,

So we can preach only of Your messages.

Bless our eyes my Lord,

So we do not prejudge blindly.

Bless our hearts my Lord,

So we can be merciful.

Bless our hands my Lord,

So we can pick up our brothers and sisters

When they fall.

Bless us my Lord The Omnipresence.

May Your glad tidings befall upon us,

THE BELOVED

CREATION OF THE

BELOVED LORD.

ACCEPT ME AS YOUR OWN

My Lord, forgive this creation

As I have traveled only for You.

My Lord, I search for Your blessings,

Your forgiveness, Your mercy, and

Your acceptance of this mind, body, and soul.

Oh my Lord, I have traveled near and far.

I have traveled all around

To only find You my Lord.

I have come upon my home

As I await Your arrival.

May You my Lord accept

This mind, body, and soul

As You come upon my door and

ACCEPT ME

AS YOUR OWN.

AWAKENED ONLY FOR MY LORD THE OMNIPOTENT

My Lord, with the sun rising upon the Earth,

May we, Your creation, awaken sin free.

As daylight reaches the humans, may we awaken

To the truth of The Omnipotent's glory,

Guiding all throughout eternity as You have placed

All the elements of nature for

Your beloved creation.

May we, Your creation, on this day awaken and

Know our beloved Omnipotent is but walking

Amongst us for the love of the creation.

My Lord, on this day, hold my hands

And let my complete soul be

AWAKENED ONLY

FOR MY LORD

THE OMNIPOTENT.

BLESSED BE
THE OMNIPRESENCE

Oh my Lord,

Accept the heartfelt prayer of this soul,

As I but awaken at dawn,

Only for You.

This dawn breaks through the dark night

And brings hope within the Earth

To each and all of Your creation.

My Lord, my Creator,

On this day,

May I, Your creation,

Ask of You to give us Your blessings

For You are but The Omnipresence.

Within Your Hands are but

The Earth, the skies, and all of the creation.

For You, oh my Lord,

In union we but say,

The Omnipresence,

The Omnipresence,

The Omnipresence,

BLESSED BE

THE OMNIPRESENCE.

BLESSED BE THE BATH OF THE CLEAN SOUL

Blessed be the dawn that brings forth

The repented, the redeemed,

And the awakened souls,

To The House of my Lord.

My Lord accepts this soul as I awaken

Sin free, pure, and clean.

My Lord holds on to the hands of all of whom

But take a bath within the repented and redeemed

Ocean of one's own confession,

Where there is only one boat,

Where the clean soul takes a journey

Through the river of purity,

Holding on to the oars of The Omnipotent.

BLESSED BE THE BATH

OF THE CLEAN SOUL.

FOREVER, ETERNALLY MINE

Oh my Lord,

Blessed be the repentance of a repented soul.

Blessings are but all this soul requires

To exist my Lord.

For eternally, I am but Yours my Lord.

Oh my Lord, my Creator,

Even when all is no more,

The Earth, the skies, and the oceans

Are all but extinct,

May the blessings of my Lord be,

FOREVER,

ETERNALLY MINE.

THE ETERNAL LIGHT OF THE OMNIPOTENT

Darkness evolves all around,

Yet fearless and determined I am

For I have the blessings of

My Lord The Omnipotent.

All around this Earth,

Fire burns within different houses,

All claiming to be the one and only eternal truth.

Oh my Lord, truth is but You.

Oh my Lord, truth is but The Right Path.

Oh my Lord, truth is but

The human blessed with humanity.

Oh my Lord, from beneath the darkness,

From above and beyond all human eyes,

My Lord's spiritual lighthouse glows and guides

All from the beginning till the end.

Through this, may I, Your creation,

Find my way back to You.

Because of this,

May I, Your creation, never go astray.

For You, may I, Your creation,

Be upon The Blessed Path,

Guided always by

THE ETERNAL LIGHT

OF THE OMNIPOTENT.

BLESSED FORGIVEN

My Lord The Omnipotent,

Guide me through this journey,

So the journey of my life begins and ends

With Your name, in Your name,

And for Your name only.

My Lord The Most Merciful,

I walk upon the road blindfolded.

Please hold my hands, so I never get lost.

Oh my Lord, be my Guide.

I see so many different routes

With Your name pasted on them.

May my eyes never be fooled

And always be open for Your Path only.

Please direct me my Lord.

My Lord, The Giver of abundance,

I wait for Your words only.

For when they come,

May my ears hear of them, and know of them,

For within these words,

Lay the blessings of my Lord.

My Lord The Most Forgiving,

With the burden of my sins within my chest,

I hold my hands up high in Your devotion.

May I walk upon

The Road of Forgiveness my Lord.

My Lord The Punisher,

Punish me so I may be awakened.

May my soul be set free from all Earthly sins.

May I find You my Lord before my last breath.

My Lord The Judge of The Judgment Day,

As nightfall approaches,

May I walk back home to my Lord, my Creator,

For I am amongst the,

BLESSED FORGIVEN.

MY FINAL RESTING PLACE

My Lord, guide me through

My final journey back home.

May The Angels up in Heaven

Guide me upon my journey.

May they guide me upon The Right Path.

Oh my Lord, may Mother Earth

Keep me within her chest.

Oh my Lord, may she give shelter to me.

Oh my Lord, may Mother Earth

Let the green grass grow under my feet,

Let the tall trees give me food,

And let the skies be my roof.

May I lay my head down

On the soft green grass.

Let it be my blanket in the cold winter nights.

During the hot summer days,

Let the skies pour cold water over my body.

Let the hot rays of the sun give me warmth

During the cold winter nights.

Oh my Lord,

My Mother Earth is my last resting place.

I rest my body in your chest oh Mother Earth,

For my life ends but my journey continues.

As my body lies in your chest,

Let my soul walk through you.

My Lord, welcome me into The House of Heaven.

My Lord, take me through The Gates of Heaven.

May I be amongst the blessed ones

Where the fountains pour soothing water

And the trees bear fruits,

Where my Creator but carries me back home,

To The House of my Creator The Omnipotent,

MY FINAL

RESTING PLACE.

FOR MY LORD
THE OMNIPRESENCE

My Lord, forgive for I have sinned,

For this body is but within the sinful oceans,

Covered by the sins and sinners.

The lands have been covered

By the bath waters of the sinners.

Your oceans are but filled with all contaminated,

Sinful waters my Lord.

The mountain breeze evolves

From the breath of the sinners my Lord.

I, Your repented creation, walk upon Mother Earth

As she is but blessed by You my Lord.

The oceans I bathe in are but

Your Heavenly waters,

Decontaminated through repentance my Lord.

The mountain breeze is but filled with love as

I sing the sweet songs of prayers for You my Lord.

For even within all the sins and sinners,

I am but free from all

The eternal, forbidden sins my Lord,

For this soul awakens only for You

My Lord, my Creator.

Forever this mind, body, and soul are but

In prostration,

In devotion,

In meditation,

For I am but the candle of hope,

FOR MY LORD

THE OMNIPRESENCE.

"MY CHILD, FEAR NOT FOR I AM BUT HERE"

My Lord The Most Forgiving,

My Lord The Most Merciful,

I, Your most devoted creation,

Prostrate to You, my Lord.

My Lord, I hear The Angels of Heaven

Blowing the trumpets announcing our last days.

Forgive me my Lord.

Forgive me my Lord.

Forgive me my Lord.

With this vow of repentance,

I watch the last sunsets of this world.

The days are ending

And the skies all around me are but getting dark.

I know the darkest part of my life

Is but in front of me.

My Lord, this devotee is not scared,

Is not frightened by the dark waves of the night,

For I know my Lord is there.

My Lord is there.

My Lord is there.

I see not, I hear not, I feel not,

But I know You are there.

I know my Lord is there.

The unknown darkness,

The unknown, frightful night

Scares me not, for I know even though,

Unknown to all, unseen to all, unheard by all,

My Lord is there.

My faith carries me

Through this wave of darkness my Lord.

My heart shows me The Path

And my beliefs keep me throughout this dark night

Steadfast for I know my Lord is there.

The calls of the unknown beast,

The calls of the fiery night,

The calls of the devil

But give me no chills

For I know my Lord is there.

The broken roads, the steep hills,

The high mountains, the rivers

That I have to cross, frighten me not,

For I know my Lord is there.

At the end of the night,

Dawn breaks open through the night skies,

Announcing daybreak is but ahead.

I see with open Hands, my Lord calls me

And says,

"MY CHILD, FEAR NOT

FOR I AM BUT HERE."

ANN MARIE RUBY

MY PRAYERS HAVE BEEN ACCEPTED

As daylight finally breaks through
After the dark nights,
I know my Lord accepts my prayers.
For all throughout the dark nights, I had never lost
Faith within my complete belief, within my Lord.
The storms of the dark nights,
The waves of the windy oceans,
Do not break my ark of faith,
For I know after all the obstacles,
Within all the hurdles and amongst all the pain,
My love for my Lord keeps me afloat.
For on this day finally, I see my faith, my belief,
And my worship land upon shore,
For on this day, I know
MY PRAYERS
HAVE BEEN ACCEPTED.

150

THE OMNIPOTENT AS MY ONLY SAVIOR

My Lord The Alpha,

My Lord The Omega,

We, Your creation, must return home

At the end of our journey.

Oh my Lord, grant us mercy.

Oh my Lord, grant us forgiveness.

My Lord, may we see the truth.

My Lord, may we find The Path.

My Lord, may we arrive

At The Door of Repentance.

May the deadly sins of life

Not grant us a home in the fearful house of Hell,

As we enter our final resting place my Lord.

Accept my repentance my Lord.

Grant me forgiveness my Lord,

For I the redeemer repent, repent, repent.

For I the redeemer take the vow of repentance.

I the redeemer take the vow of redemption,

For with this redemption I the saved

Accept The Judge of Judgment Day,

THE OMNIPOTENT

AS MY ONLY SAVIOR.

MY LORD IS THE CREATOR, FOR MY LORD IS THE DESTRUCTOR

Oh my Lord,

You are but my faith.

Oh my Lord,

You are but my ways.

Oh my Lord,

You are but all the knowledge.

Oh my Lord,

You are but of all

That is above and beyond.

You are my Earth, my Heaven, my Home.

Oh my Lord,

I am but the human.

Oh my Lord,

I am but Your creation.

Oh my Lord,

I breathe but with Your breath.

As Your breath gives all life,

It is but Your breath that shall take all for,

MY LORD IS

THE CREATOR,

FOR MY LORD IS

THE DESTRUCTOR.

HERE IT BEGINS, NOW IT BEGINS

The forbidden sins, the unhidden secrets,

The open acceptance of the sins,

Bring forth land after land

Filled with nothing but sinners.

The invisible shield,

The secret door of The Lord's curse shall be open.

Nothing but shall remain

For with the acceptance of the sins,

The curse shall befall on all creation.

May I, Your true devotee,

Not be amongst the cursed.

May I be with my Lord before all this but begins.

If my destiny brings me on to this time,

Forgive me my Lord.

Save me within Your grace.

Forgive me, forgive me, forgive me my Lord.

May I be amongst the chosen ones.

May I be amongst the pure.

May I be the chosen child of my Lord,

For I the sinner repent, repent, repent,

Repent, repent, repent, repent,

For with this repentance, I the pure hear the sounds

From all around the Earth,

As all the creation but run, hide,

And try to find safety amongst each other,

Within their sins.

I hear the End of World is but upon us,

For the sound gets louder and louder.

It is the sound of the End of Time,

For everything that but begins must also end.

HERE IT BEGINS,

NOW IT BEGINS.

THE MERCIFUL

My Lord, my Creator,

Within Your Hands, everything but is,

And it is within Your Hands,

That everything but shall end.

You are The First and You are also The Last.

You are The Alpha.

You are The Omega.

Within Your commands, everything but begins.

Within Your commands, everything but shall end.

Where there is no hope, there is but one.

Where there is no light, there is but one.

You are The First for You are also The Last.

Protect us as we the dead shall be resurrected.

Guide us as we the living must return.

For You are Wisdom.

You are Knowledge.

You are The Giver.

You are The Sustainer.

You are The Preserver.

You are The Protector.

Within Your commands, everything but shall end.

Where there is no hope, there is but one.

Where there is no light, there is but one.

We call upon You for You are

The Merciful, The Merciful,

THE MERCIFUL.

THE HOUSE UP
IN HEAVEN

Heaven is but

The Home, The House of my Creator.

Up in Heaven, You but reside.

I, Your creation, walk upon the Earth.

As I roam from land to land,

I call upon you oh Heaven, oh Heaven,

The House of my Creator, where are you?

How do I find you?

Guide me.

Show me.

Direct me for I search only for you.

My mind, body, and soul know

There is but only one house I must find

And it is The House up in Heaven.

Guide me to you.

Show me how I, a mere creation,

May come upon your door.

For with all of my prayers and all of my soul,

I only have one wish, to find you.

My prayers but knock upon the glass door

That but separates you from me.

My prayers reach The Door of Heaven

For I feel the glass door shattering.

Crystal clear water droplets fall on top of my head

As the glass shatters

And becomes the holy water.

The holy water of Heaven bathes me, cleanses me,

And prepares me for my entry

To The House of Heaven.

With the last bath, clean, and fresh scented I am

As I walk into the house

My Creator has built for me,

For I know it is my final resting place,

The home I have dreamt about.

Today, may my prayers be answered

For with this bath,

My mind, body, and soul rejuvenate and

Awaken again, as the child of my Lord.

For with this knowledge,

I see The Doors open once again for me as I enter

The Home of my Creator,

THE HOUSE UP

IN HEAVEN.

MOTHER EARTH

My Lord, may I, Your creation, be safe and secure

Within Mother Earth,

For I know within her chest,

She hides all of her children.

May I not divide between the children of this

Mother for she gives me food and water,

Sheltering me within her chest

As she but shelters all of her children.

My Lord, may I give love and care

To all of the children of Mother Earth.

My Lord, may I find within

My mind, body, and soul,

Forgiveness, mercy, and blessings

For all of the children of this Mother,

We all but know as,

MOTHER EARTH.

THE HANDS OF MY LORD

My Lord, I the sinner fall as

You but pick me up.

My Lord, I the repenter repent as

You but accept my prayers.

My Lord, I the sick cry as

You but heal me.

My Lord, I the weak fall prey as

You but protect me.

My Lord, I, Your child, call upon You

At every turn of my life.

When I drown, I call upon You.

When I fall, I call upon You.

When I sin, I call upon You.

As all the creation but ask,

"Who but is our Lord?"

I answer, "I know our Lord

Is but The Omnipotent."

For I know from the moment

I was created till the End of Time,

It is my Lord, my Creator who but protects me.

The greatest powers

That have but protected the creation,

Throughout eternity

Are but,

THE HANDS OF MY LORD.

MY LORD
BUT ACCEPTS ME

Oh my Lord, may my prayers reach Your Door.

My Lord, this devotee calls upon You, only You.

I search for You from dawn to dusk with hope

I shall but find You.

The roads leading to You have thorns laid

Upon them which I pick up one by one.

I pray along the way,

May no one else find all this hardship

Trying to reach You.

I climb the steep hills, never giving up hope

For I know You are there.

As I reach the gates my Lord,

All but stop and question me.

As I touch the gates and pray,

My Lord, my Creator, I only worship You.

Teardrops but fall and all my pain and wounds

Start to create a veil,

For I hide my prayers from this world.

I only ask, seek, and knock upon Your Door.

May my Lord open the gates for me.

May my Lord's Path be my path.

My Lord, hear my prayers, see my prayers, answer

My prayers for this devotee only worships You.

My Lord, open the gates, come for me.

Let The Heavens above know of it.

Let the Earth beneath know of it.

For on this day,

My Lord, remove all the obstacles of eternity.

For today, the barriers of all that is unknown

Be removed.

For with complete faith,

I know,

MY LORD

BUT ACCEPTS ME.

WATER OF LIFE

Oh Mother Earth, cleanse me.

Oh Mother Earth, cleanse me.

Oh Mother Earth, cleanse me

From the sins of this world.

My Lord The Omnipotent,

I purify myself from all Earthly sins.

Oh Mother Earth,

As the water but touches my body,

Cleanse me with your pure holy water.

Oh Heavenly water,

I cannot travel to you,

But may Mother Earth cleanse me,

For I take shelter in her from all sins.

Oh Heavenly water,

Cleanse me from all Earthly sins.

I pray to You my Lord,

May all of my sins be washed away

For we only have a day.

With every breath I pray,

Cleanse me oh holy water

Of Earth and Heavens above.

Purify my body my Lord.

May the holy water of Heaven

Flow through my body.

Wash me.

Wash me.

Wash me oh Heavenly water.

My Lord The Omnipotent,

I cleanse myself.

I cleanse myself.

I cleanse myself.

Let the water flow and wash away

All the dirt off of my body.

Let all the Earthly sins be washed away.

Oh the rivers of Heaven,

Wash away all of my sins.

May my sins not touch other souls

As they put their feet within the rivers.

May my sins not touch or burn them.

Oh holy water, cleanse me.

I take a bath for You my Lord.

In Your name, may I live on this Earth, sin free.

In Your name, my Lord The Omnipotent,

I bathe in the

WATER OF LIFE.

ANSWERED BY
THE OMNIPOTENT

My Lord, my Creator,

My Lord The Alpha, my Lord The Omega,

All but began within Your commands,

For all but ends within Your commands.

My Lord The Creator of everything,

My Lord The Final Judge of all creation,

Hand in hand we hold as all humans but unite

Within one final prayer, for our love,

Of our Lord The Omnipotent.

We the humans awaken within one house,

The final house of all the creation.

We stand united within one prayer, watching

The Heavenly Lights guide from above as

We know the united prayers of all creation are but

ANSWERED BY

THE OMNIPOTENT.

THE BLESSED SUN
IS BUT BORN

Dusk but approaches,

Announcing the arrival of the dark nights.

My Lord, my Creator,

Hold on to my hands as I but walk

Through the dark nights.

My Lord, my Creator,

May I, Your creation, but not go astray,

Or fall prey within these dark nights.

My Lord, my Creator,

Throughout this time,

Guide me through my dreams,

As I know You are but The Merciful,

And The Forgiving.

Oh my Lord,

May Your given dreams, and Your given visions,

Be my guide until dawn breaks through,

For I know as dawn breaks open

Through the night sky, it is then,

To guide all throughout eternity,

THE BLESSED SUN

IS BUT BORN.

THE OMNIPRESENCE, THE OMNIPRESENCE, THE OMNIPRESENCE

The Earth but is flooded

With the sins of the sinners my Lord,

For all around me, there is but the temptation

Of the mind, the body, and the soul.

For wherever the eyes but fall, the sins,

And the sinners but rule my Lord.

For where there is might,

There is a call for the wrong to be called the right.

My Lord, the Earth but shatters,

The rivers but flood,

The mountains but erupt,

For there is nothing left to save the humans

Or The Angels.

Within The Heavens above and Earth beneath,

All sacred books but seek for answers my Lord.

For all around, there is nothing left but the might

And rights of the sinners and their sins.

Oh my Lord,

Where do I but find hope and blessings?

Who do I but pray to?

And how do I but pray my Lord?

With all my faith and all my courage,

I wait at the river bend of all the sinners and

All the accumulated sins of this Earth my Lord.

Oh my Lord, my Creator,

Like a bolt of lightning

From beneath the oceans of the Earth and

Under the guided stars of Heavens above,

To carry all back to The Path of The Omnipotent,

Rises,

THE OMNIPRESENCE,

THE OMNIPRESENCE,

THE OMNIPRESENCE.

BLESSED BE
THE OMNIPRESENCE

My Lord, my Creator,

May there be forgiveness.

May there be mercy.

May there be blessings.

Blessed be,

Blessed be,

Blessed be.

For when the humans but first open their eyes,

My Lord but says,

"Blessed Be."

For all humans and Angels above,

My Lord but cries as my Lord repeats,

"Blessed be the repented.

Blessed be the repentance.

Blessed be the awakened soul

Who but seeks the blessings of The Omnipotent."

For within Heavens above, my Lord is.

Even on Earth beneath, my Lord is.

For now,

All awakened humans unite,

And say in union,

BLESSED BE

THE OMNIPRESENCE.

THE BLESSED CHILDREN OF THE OMNIPOTENT

Within dark nights, we hold on to each other.

Within the hurdles, we light the candles of hope.

Within the unknown and unseen storms,

We become an anchor for each other.

For eternally throughout time,

We have been walking upon

The Path of The Omnipotent.

May evil not but enter our ears.

May evil not but reach our eyes.

May evil not but touch our lips.

For we only ask,

For we only seek,

For we only knock,

Upon The Omnipotent's Door.

For we have within our mind, body, and soul,

The love for our Lord.

Forever we have been reciting to our Lord,

"May my love for You and Your love for me,

Protect me throughout eternity."

For we are,

THE BLESSED

CHILDREN OF

THE OMNIPOTENT.

FOR YOU ARE THE OMNIPRESENCE, BLESSED BE

I search for You within the skies.

I search for You within this Earth.

I search for You within the oceans.

I search for You on top of the mountain.

"Where do I find You?"

I ask myself over and over again.

I know within my faith,

I find You.

Within all the blessings,

I find You.

Within the past,

I find You.

In the present,

I find You.

In the far future You travel,

Even though I cannot.

For I know,

You were there,

You are here,

And You shall always be,

FOR YOU ARE

THE OMNIPRESENCE,

BLESSED BE.

OUR SAVING GRACE, THE OMNIPRESENCE

Dark times but come upon this Earth,

Where Your humans cry for the glimpse of hope.

My Lord, the nights are longer and

The days are but darker, and windy.

This creation tries to keep the lanterns glowing,

For all my Lord.

The sinners and their sins,

Are but spreading all over the globe.

The dark souls are but awakening

With might my Lord.

This creation will keep the lanterns glowing,

For all of the spiritual souls

To find their ways back to You my Lord.

Within the Earth,

I shall walk with my lanterns glowing,

Within my hands, my Lord.

Within the dark oceans,

I shall float within my ark of faith,

Always holding on to my lantern my Lord.

For I know from beneath the Earth,

Even within the dark blue oceans,

Appearing like the bolt of lightning,

From the skies above,

Comes upon the humans,

Our hope, our blessings, our answered prayers,

OUR SAVING GRACE,

THE OMNIPRESENCE.

THE HURDLES
LIFE BUT BRINGS

My Lord The Omnipotent,

My Lord The Omnipresence,

I am but Your creation,

Confused and lost,

Stranded, alone with nothing but hurdles,

Ahead and behind.

Oh my Lord,

Guide me through these hurdles.

Oh my Lord,

Let there be light.

Oh my Lord,

Let there be knowledge.

Oh my Lord,

May I be able to knock and open

The blocked doors.

Oh my Lord,

May I be able to seek and find

The path of my quest.

Oh my Lord,

May the unknown and unseen hurdles,

Unknown to me yet all but is known to You,

Not but bury me.

My Lord, I, Your devoted creation, shall travel

Through all of the obstacles life but gives.

I only ask, seek, and knock for the answer.

How do I, Your devoted creation, but

Find myself out of

THE HURDLES

LIFE BUT BRINGS?

REPENTED, REDEEMED, AND AWAKENED SOUL

Oh my Lord, upon this stormy day, I ask

May I be safe and protected always

By The Omnipotent's

Mercy, blessings, and forgiveness.

May I know how, why, and when to repent.

May I repent from the mind, the body,

And the soul.

May my repentance and prayers be accepted

As I but awaken sin free, pure, and clean.

May the sinners and their sins

Not drown my repented, redeemed,

And awakened soul.

May the sinners and their sins

Not bury me.

May the sinners and their sins flying

Within the skies not take me away floating.

May I be there standing above all
As Your sin free, pure, and clean,
REPENTED, REDEEMED,
AND AWAKENED SOUL.

THE CANDLES
OF REPENTANCE

Within The House of my Lord,

There is but no place

For the sins or their beholders, the sinners.

For as I end up in front of The Blessed Door,

There shining like the candles,

Glowing so bright,

Throughout the days,

And throughout the nights,

Are but the holy commandments,

Of my Lord.

For it is then these commandments

Shall but take life.

For just like me, the commandments

Too shall awaken,

For they will block off The Path for me,

For they will retell my stories throughout eternity,

Only for me to but remember.

For then it is but my awakening realization,

My own acceptance,

My own confession,

From my mind, body, and soul,

As I but awaken through my own

Repentance and redemption.

For only then,

I shall find an entry,

Through The Door of Forgiveness

As I but awaken through,

THE CANDLES

OF REPENTANCE.

THE OMNIPOTENT, THE OMNIPRESENCE, THE OMNISCIENCE

Blessed be the prayers of a blessed soul.

Blessed be the repentance of a blessed soul.

For with this repentance, I redeem,

And with this redemption, I take a bath,

And be sin free, pure, and clean.

Blessed be the repentance.

Blessed be the redemption of a redeemed soul

Who takes a bath within

The complete truth of The Omnipotent.

Blessed be The Omnipresence.

Blessed be The Omniscience.

Blessed be my Lord.

Accept the prayers

Of this human mind, body, and soul

As I awaken sin free,

ANN MARIE RUBY

Washed within the prayers of my repentance,

My redemption, and my awakening.

Accept me my Lord.

Accept my prayers my Lord.

Accept this blessed soul

As I awaken sin free, pure, and clean,

Your creation, Your complete devotee.

I ask You my Creator on this day,

Accept my prayers which I only ask of You.

Accept me my Lord.

Accept my prayers my Lord.

Accept this prayer I recite upon this day my Lord.

Grant my wish my Lord.

Grant this pure soul, the pure wish

That comes from my mind, body, and soul.

Accept my Lord.

Accept my prayers my Lord.

Grant me my one wish, my Lord, my Creator,

THE OMNIPOTENT,

THE OMNIPRESENCE,

THE OMNISCIENCE.

190

BLESSED WITHIN PEACE

My Lord but created this blessed race

We but call the humans.

May this race be blessed as we are the blessed.

May this group stand for each other

As we are all but one.

May this group in union walk

From birth until death,

As we all share the one highway.

May we the life travelers guide all

Throughout our journey of life.

From the beginning

Until the end of this highway,

There are but travelers who have a one-way map.

May we in union walk for each other as,

There is but one road, one entry, and one exit

Which are but marked in peace.

ANN MARIE RUBY

May this journey through life also be,
BLESSED WITHIN
PEACE.

RESURRECT YOUR CREATION

Oh my Lord,

I give You my mind, body, and soul.

Oh my Lord,

Within my human mind, body, and soul,

Let there be no trace of evil.

Oh my Lord,

Let this sin free, repented, and redeemed

Mind, body, and soul be awakened.

Oh my Lord,

Let this ocean of life wash me.

Oh my Lord,

Let the sun above glow upon my resurrected body.

Oh my Lord,

I know my mind, body, and soul

Only awaken for You,

As You are The First and You are The Last.

You are but my Lord, my Creator for I know,

You are The Omnipotent who but can,

RESURRECT YOUR

CREATION.

BLESSED ARK
OF THE SEA

My Lord, my Creator,

Sinners are but we who have fallen.

Oh my Lord, my Creator,

Pious are but Your chosen guides

Who travel near and travel far,

Only to guide Your lost and stranded souls.

Oh my Lord, The Ark of Your devoted guides

But stands and waits for one and for all.

From Heavens above, the stars twinkle to guide us.

From oceans beneath,

Await the miracles of the seas,

As they but guide all back to You.

My Lord, my Creator,

May I, Your devotee, be guided first,

For then, may I but guide all the lost and stranded,

Who but ask, seek, and knock

As we all but wait

For The Omnipotent's

BLESSED ARK

OF THE SEA.

MY PILGRIMAGE IS BUT COMPLETE

My Lord, my Creator,

May my life be a complete journey

Through Your commandments.

For You, I devote this blessed life,

To be in complete devotion of You,

My Lord, my Creator.

Oh my Lord, may my life be a sacred journal

For all of whom seek the same path.

I pray my Lord,

Let all devotees taking a journey

Within this path not be lost,

For we the pilgrims

Only do this pilgrimage for You,

On Your Given Path.

My Lord, let the devotion

Of this devotee be accepted.

Accept my devotion my Lord,

For it is then

I know

MY PILGRIMAGE

IS BUT COMPLETE.

I AM BUT THE JUDGED

My Lord, my Creator,

Let this mind, body, and soul not fall prey

To the temptations of this life.

May I not fall prey to my weakness

Of these worldly sins.

May I be strong and blessed within

Your mercy, forgiveness, and blessings.

May I only land upon Your Blessed Path,

Within Your given words,

Your given commandments of life.

May my words be only from You.

May my hands only do good.

May my Earthly body be sin free, pure, and clean.

Oh my Lord, may my soul be immersed

Within Your love.

From dawn through dusk through dawn,

May I, Your creation, be only Yours.

May I not divide amongst Your creation,

Your Path,

Your words,

For You are but The Judge, for

I AM BUT THE JUDGED.

THROUGHOUT THE JOURNEY OF LIFE

My Lord, my Creator,

Prayers are but the sacred doors to eternity.

Words within the prayers are but the keys

Of the sacred doors.

The human reciting the prayers

But opens these sacred doors.

Oh my Lord,

Blessed be the night,

Blessed be the day,

Blessed be the time,

And blessed be the hour,

A human but awakens and finds oneself.

Within each individual soul is

But hidden our individual key to Heaven.

For with this key, we the humans

But open the doors to our life's journey.

This key but opens and closes

The doors to health, wealth, and wisdom.

Oh my Lord, my Creator,

I ask, seek, and knock upon Your Door.

May I the beholder of my key

Not lose my only hope,

THROUGHOUT

THE JOURNEY OF LIFE.

YOU ARE BUT MY SAVING GRACE

Let the skies not shower us with sins as

You become our umbrella to protect us

From all evil

As You are but

The Omnipotent Complete.

May the Earth beneath not bury us within sins,

As You are but the ground

For You are but

The Omnipotent Complete.

Let the oceans not drown us

Within the sinful waters as You are but

The Ark picking up all of Your creation,

As You are but

The Omnipotent Complete.

On this day, my mind, body, and soul but ask You

My Lord, my Creator,

Protect us throughout eternity

For You are

The Omnipotent Complete.

Within You, I find my protection for

YOU ARE BUT MY

SAVING GRACE.

THE DOOR OF HOPE

Blessed be the days ahead of all patient souls for

We the repented, redeemed, and awakened souls

But patiently wait for justice and protection.

We seek justice and protection from all evil

And wrong-doings of these humanly doings.

Blessed be the patience of a devoted soul,

As throughout the dark times,

It is only patience that but guides all,

To and through,

THE DOOR OF HOPE.

THE BLESSED SACRED PATH OF MY LORD

My Lord The Omnipotent,

Forgive this soul for all Earthly sins committed,

But repented, redeemed, and awakened from.

May this mind, body, and soul be awakened

Sin free, my Lord.

May all the hurdles that land upon my path

Be removed and may this creation have a blessed

Sacred journey through life.

Within my traveler's bag of life, I have

My repentance, blessings, and faith as my guide.

May I, Your creation, be a sin free, sacred soul,

As I travel through the

THE BLESSED SACRED

PATH OF MY LORD.

COMPLETE SELF TO MY LORD, MY CREATOR

My Lord The Most Merciful,

The One who removes all pain and sorrows,

I call upon You my Lord

At a time of distress and need.

My Lord, all around is pain and sorrow,

Darkness taking over.

Your true devotees are waiting for You

On this dark, cloudy road,

Never losing hope for my Lord is there.

My faith will never break but get stronger.

I know You give me pain for

You love me the most.

At the crossroad, I am waiting for

Your guiding lights to guide,

For I know You but guide all of Your creation.

Hands spread out You but have for me.

ANN MARIE RUBY

With complete love,

I give my

COMPLETE SELF TO

MY LORD, MY CREATOR.

MY CREATOR
THE ALPHA,
THE OMEGA

My Lord, forgive me for my sins.

I walk alone on This Path my Lord,

For I am trying to find Your House.

This Path is full of curves and detours,

But I am trying to stay on Your Route.

Your messages keep getting mixed up

With so many who are trying to send

Mixed messages from all over.

Pick me up my Lord when I fall.

Hold my hands my Lord,

So I stay steadfast on Your Path.

Guide me my Lord when I am lost.

My Lord, leave a light on within Your House,

So I may find Your Door.

I walk through a tunnel of light

That swirls and curves,

But I see the light You have left on for me.

My Lord, You have been asking all Your creation

To walk back to Your House.

The eternal love for You but pulls me

Toward You my Lord.

The patience You show all

Keeps my belief forever so strong.

My Lord, I beg on Your mercy for

You are The Only One I ask guidance from.

My Lord, I am the sinner who knocks

On Your Door for forgiveness.

Hear my knock my Lord,

For You have said, "Knock and I shall open."

My Lord, I am here now at Your Door,

At The Door of Forgiveness.

Oh my Lord, forgive me now for my sins,

For I know You are

MY CREATOR

THE ALPHA,

THE OMEGA.

THE OMNIPOTENT IS BUT FOUND

Blessed be the prayers of a repented soul.

Blessed be the prayers of a redeemed soul.

Blessed be the prayers of an awakened soul.

Blessed be the human who but repents, redeems,

And awakens for the love of The Omnipotent.

Blessed be the dawn

That but witnessed a repenter's repentance.

Blessed be the dusk

That but witnessed a repenter's repentance.

For even when all but ends and nothing is but left,

The repentance, the redemption, and the awakened

Soul of a human but exist throughout time.

For within this circle,

THE OMNIPOTENT IS

BUT FOUND.

PRAYER IS BUT COMPLETE

My Lord, blessed be the prayers of a blessed soul.

May this seeker's prayers be accepted

By You my Lord.

For I shall only knock upon Your Door my Lord,

Not the doors of any human.

For I only ask my Lord, my Creator, for all the

Guidance, blessings, mercy, and forgiveness.

For I know I am but a creation of The Creator,

The Omnipotent, The Omnipresence.

For I know the prayers are but answered as,

When a true prayer is uttered from the lips,

Heard by the ears, and is from

The mind, the body and the soul,

Then it is true, this

PRAYER IS BUT

COMPLETE.

PROTECTED THROUGHOUT ETERNITY

Oh my Lord,

The days are dark, and nights are darker.

The sky is filling up with thick heavy clouds.

High pitched screams

From the beast pierces our ears.

All around us, the beast roams around freely,

Lurking around in search of lost souls for his prey.

My Lord The Most High, keep us in Your prayers

And bestow Your blessings upon us.

May Your True Angels always guide us.

May Your twinkling lights

Keep the beast afar from us.

May Your guiding stars arrive amongst us

Before the beast.

May we, Your true devotees, be able

To fight the beast when needed.

May Your love for us and our love for You

Be our true protection from all evil,

Known and unknown, seen or unseen they may be.

With this prayer, may I the devotee be completely

PROTECTED

THROUGHOUT

ETERNITY.

OMNIPOTENT, THE FINAL CHAPTER MUST BE

My Lord The Omnipresence,

Give us strength to withstand the evolution.

My Lord, with this transition,

We shall all but reunite with our Creator.

My Lord, may we not be lost within the turmoil

As the beast attacks with fury

Through this transition.

My Lord, the sun flares,

Sparking fire all around us,

Warning to be aware of the beastly attacks.

My Lord, the moon but is getting red

As it pours blood all over the Earth

In search of the beast.

My Lord, the rivers and lands are lost

Within agony as the beast

But devours the air and water vehicles.

With an empty glare,

Humans are but devouring

Each other as evil but controls them.

Boats have come ashore claiming

To be of Yours my Lord.

The dragon and the beast roam around

To devour Your creation my Lord.

As the sun sets and all is

But being devoured by darkness,

We call upon our Lord The Omnipotent.

Oh come, oh come our Lord The Omnipotent,

Oh come, oh come our Lord The Omnipotent.

Come with Your Holy Ark

Oh our Lord The Omnipotent,

So we the children may be aboard.

For all but is within Your Hands oh my Lord.

For with this evolution,

OMNIPOTENT,

THE FINAL CHAPTER

MUST BE.

ABOUT THE AUTHOR

I am an unknown person who lived the struggles, overcame the obstacles, as I have endured the pain and joy of life as they landed upon my door.

I like to be the unknown face to whom all can relate. I want you to see your face in the mirror when you search for me, not mine. For if it is my face in the mirror, then my friend you see a stranger. The unknown face is there so you see only yourself, your struggles, your achievements as you cross the journey of life. I want to be the face of a white, black, and brown, as well as the love we are always searching eternally for. If this world would have allowed, I would have distributed all of my books, to you with my own hands as a gift and a message from a friend. I have taken pen to paper to spread peace throughout this Earth. My sacred soul has found peace within herself. May I through my words bring peace and solace within your soul.

You have my name and know I will always be there for anyone who seeks me. My home is Washington State, USA, yet I travel all around the world to find you, the human with humanity. Aside from my books, I love writing openly on my blog. Through this blog journey, I am available to all throughout this world. Come, let us journey together and spread positivity, as I take you on a positive journey through my blog.

For more information about any one of my books, or to read my blog posts, subscribe to my blog on my website, www.annmarieruby.com. Follow me on social media, @AnnahMariahRuby on Twitter, @TheAnnMarieRuby on Facebook, @ann_marie_ruby on Instagram, and @TheAnnMarieRuby on Pinterest.

217

MY SPIRITUAL COLLECTION

I have published four books of original inspirational quotations:

Spiritual Travelers:
Life's Journey From The Past To The Present
For The Future

Spiritual Messages:
From A Bottle

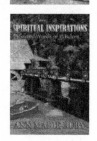

Spiritual Journey:
Life's Eternal Blessings

Spiritual Inspirations:
Sacred Words Of Wisdom

For all of you whom have requested my complete inspirational quotations, I have my complete ark of inspiration, I but call:

Spiritual Ark:
The Enchanted Journey Of Timeless Quotations

Do you believe in dreams? For within each individual dream, there is a hidden message and a miracle interlinked. Learn the spiritual, scientific, religious, and philosophical aspects of dreams. Walk with me as you travel through forty nights, through the pages of my book:

Spiritual Lighthouse:
The Dream Diaries Of Ann Marie Ruby

When there was no hope, I found hope within these sacred words of prayers, I but call songs. Within this book, I have for you, 100 very sacred prayers:

Spiritual Songs:
Letters From My Chest

I have another sacred prayer book with 123 prayers for all humans with humanity:

Spiritual Songs II:
Blessings From A Sacred Soul

SPIRITUAL SONGS: LETTERS FROM MY CHEST

From the first sight of dawn till the first sight of dusk, and throughout the dark nights, may the sweet songs of prayers be within our mind, body, and soul. For me, prayers are but my saving grace. Within each word, my sacred soul seeks peace and serenity. Within all the pages of this book, I have my blessings sent your way. Within my first prayer book, *Spiritual Songs: Letters From My Chest*, I also have 100 blessed prayers written within her pages. May you find my blessings within her pages too. Here are two prayers from my first prayer book.

May you find hope within these prayers as I had written one for the first sight of dawn and one for the first sight of dusk. As I sit and watch dawn come upon the Earth, I always say, "Glory be to my Lord." At the first sight of dusk, I always have within my lips, "May we, the creation, await and light up each house one by one, as we carry the candles of hope."

From my blessed book, I give you my sacred prayers. May you find peace and serenity within them as I but have found.

Blessings,

Ann Marie Ruby

GLORY BE TO MY LORD

My Lord, as dawn breaks open

Through the night sky,

May I, Your devotee, only worship You.

My Lord, with this first sight of light,

May I, Your devotee, only worship You.

My Lord, after the dark night's struggle,

The sparkling array of the morning light

Glorifies the Earth.

On this day, may I, Your devotee,

Only worship You.

My Lord, as the sun reaches through

To each and all of Your creation,

May we, the creation, say in union,

"GLORY BE TO MY LORD."

CANDLES OF HOPE

My Lord,

With the sun setting in Your vast sky,

The Earth but is in the dark.

May I, Your devotee,

Be there with a candle in my hand.

My Lord,

As the night sky but turns dark with

Your moon trying to peek through to give us hope,

May I, Your devotee,

Be there with a candle in my hand.

My Lord,

As house after house

But turns dark, searching for light,

May I, Your devotee, be the light bearer

With a candle in my hand.

My Lord,

As Your moon and twinkling stars

Try to send the message of Your sun's birth,

As all but watch out for the birth of Your sun,

May we, the creation,

Await and light up each house one by one

As we carry

The

CANDLES OF HOPE.

Made in the USA
Las Vegas, NV
14 June 2023

73459287R00142